NEW IDEAS IN DEFENSIVE PLAY IN BRIDGE

by HELGE VINJE

Introduction by

TERENCE REESE

Cornerstone Library
Published by Simon & Schuster
New York

Contents

Foreword

by William B. Herseth
International Master and Editor of *Bridge in Norway*

In 1959 the publication of *The Distribution Signal*, by Helge Vinje, aroused considerable attention in all Scandinavian bridge journals. This book, in fact, introduced an entirely new approach to defensive play, based on the exchange of information by signalling. The new theories had been developed by the author and other members of the Academic Bridge Club at the University of Oslo, a club which has provided Norway with a great many of her leading international players.

One of the brand new ideas launched in this book was the distributional lead, subsequently presented as a new convention by Jan Wohlin in his book *The Lead*, published in 1964. These leads, however, were later to be known in the USA as Journalist Leads, launched by *The Bridge Journal*, the first number of which appeared in 1963.

Other innovations included the use of distribution signals on sequence leads, likewise adopted by Journalist, and a new variant of the suit preference signal, later adopted in the 1963 edition of *Goren's Bridge Complete*.

This brief survey of past events has a two-fold purpose: first to identify Vinje's theories on signalling, based on the two-card difference principle, and further developed in his new book; secondly, to show that these ideas have already proved sufficiently attractive and advanced to be adopted on a well-nigh worldwide scale.

However, whereas Vinje's first book dealt primarily with distribution signals, his theories have now been enlarged to encompass the entire area of signalling technique. This new book, I am sure, will be welcomed on all sides as a landmark in the development of defensive play.

Introduction

by Terence Reese

New bidding theories turn up every week, but how many advances have there been in the technique of play during the last thirty years? Suit preference signals, certainly; beyond that, very little, although, as William Herseth remarks in his Foreword, some of the ideas contained in the present book have previously been published in Norway and adopted under different names.

Some of Vinje's notions are complicated, but most are simple and brilliant. For example, everyone is familiar with this situation in defence against no-trumps:

```
                  x x x
  A J x x                        10 x x
                  K Q
```

West leads low to the 10 and King and later obtains the lead. Should he crack out the Ace or try to find partner's entry, in case declarer's holding is K Q x? Vinje presents an ingenious solution, as a result of which the defenders need never go wrong.

And with all the debate about leading Ace or King from a suit headed by A K, isn't it remarkable that no one has thought of a much better scheme, whereby the leader shows his count – Ace when he has A K x x, King when he holds A K x x x?

In editing the English text I have applied the same test as to my own books: if a sentence or paragraph adds nothing in an instructive way, cut it out. Helge Vinje has borne with fortitude the omission of his best oratorical flights.

PART ONE

Design for Signalling

THE RIGHT ATTITUDE

Defence is partnership par excellence. To reduce errors, the partners must adopt a far more sophisticated system of signalling than is generally practised. Such a system will undoubtedly demand a greater intellectual effort, but apart from the advantage gained, defence will prove far more interesting.

The first necessity is to develop a good signalling system. The question naturally arises: what sort of signals do we need to improve our co-operation in defence? The answer is obvious: we need *informative* signals. A signalling system should in general give information, not commands. Our signalling system conveys information equally about length and strength. At first we concentrate on length.

DISTRIBUTION SIGNALS

Every suit holding, self-evidently, is either odd or even. A void counts as even, so the main possibilities are:

    0 – 2 – 4 – 6 – even numbers
    1 – 3 – 5 – 7 – odd numbers.

Here is a simple fact of life: every suit of 13 cards must be distributed round the table in the proportion of three odds and one even, or three evens and one odd. It follows that if you know the parity of three hands, odd or even, you can estimate the fourth.

```
                        North
                        x x x
     West                                    East
     x x x               South
```

South is declarer.

West and dummy together hold six cards in the suit. The seven cards in the East and South hands must be distributed in such a way that there is an even number in one hand and an odd number in the other. Now, if West discovers by signalling that East holds an even number in the suit, he knows South must have an odd number, and if East is odd, South must be even.

When you know the type (odd or even) in a particular suit it will usually be an easy matter to decide the exact number – either two or four, three or five, and so on. This is called the 'two-card difference principle'.

Sometimes a single signal from partner, in conjunction with the bidding, will illuminate the declarer's complete hand pattern. For example:

South	North
1 ♠	2 ♣
2NT	3 ♠
4 ♠	pass

By bidding 2NT before landing in Four Spades South indicates that he has a balanced hand, probably containing five spades. If, through a signal, a defender can place South with an even number of clubs his likely hand pattern is 5 – 3 – 3 – 2. With any four-card suit apart from spades he would probably not have rebid 2NT.

A good system of signalling must fulfil three requirements:

The signal must work against both no-trump and suit contracts.

The very first card must, so far as possible, tell the story.

The signal must not be upset by declarer's use of deceptive cards.

The basic rule

High – low shows even: 2 – 4 – 6
Low – high shows odd: 1 – 3 – 5

The exact length of the suit is shown by leading, playing, or discarding in this order:

2-card suit: high – low
4-card suit: next lowest – lowest
6-card suit: third lowest – lowest
3-card suit: lowest – next lowest
5-card suit: lowest – next lowest
7-card suit: lowest – third lowest

The first card indicates the distributional type (odd or even); the second card confirms the distributional type and indicates the exact length of the suit.

When the first card played by a defender is an attempt to win the trick (or similar) he signals if possible on the next round and this signal relates to *the remaining cards, not the original holding*.

```
                    North
                    8 3
West                                   East
Q 10 6 5                               A J 4 2
                    South
                    K 9 7
```

South is playing a no-trump contract.

West leads the 6, indicating high-low for an even number. East wins the trick with the Ace. When returning the suit he plays the 2, indicating low-high for his three remaining cards. South plays the 9, West winning with the 10. West now knows the exact distribution of the suit, and also that South holds the King. (This is obvious since East played the Ace on the opening lead.) West, in the lead once again, now completes his signal by playing the 5, which confirms high-low for a four-card suit. Had he played the Queen, this might indicate an opening lead from Q 10 6, and East would not have been in possession of all the necessary information. However, if West wanted East to win the last trick in the suit, he would have to play the Queen on the third round.

```
                    North
                    Q 5
West                                East
J 10 9 7                            (1) K 6 4 3
                                    (2) K 6 3
                    South
                    (1) A 8 2
                    (2) A 8 4 2
```

South is playing a no-trump contract.

West leads the Jack, dummy covers with the Queen, East plays the King, and South heads with the Ace. When West next leads this suit, East must indicate how many cards he has left. In the case of Alternative 1 shown above he plays the 3 (low-high), indicating three remaining cards, and this enables West to cash the rest of the suit. In the case of Alternative 2 East plays the 6 (high-low), indicating two remaining cards, and West knows that the suit will not run.

The rule of fourteen

The rule of fourteen is an extension of the outmoded rule of eleven. It enables the partner to judge how many higher cards are held by the player giving the signal.

In signalling, either by a lead, a play, or a discard, the rule of fourteen operates as follows:

The thirteen cards in a suit are numbered from 2 to 14 (Ace). We subtract the number of the signalling card from fourteen, and this will tell us how many cards there are higher than the one played. The rules for signalling indicate how many higher cards are held by the defender who is signalling.

We know how many higher cards are held in dummy's hand and in our own hand, and consequently we know how many higher cards declarer holds.

If the distributional signal shows:

Three-card suit – subtract the signalling card from 12
Four-card suit – subtract the signalling card from 12
Five-card suit – subtract the signalling card from 10
Six-card suit – subtract the signalling card from 11

The rule of fourteen simplifies the procedure for counting the length of the suit where doubt exists as to whether the signalling card shows an even or an odd number.

```
                        North
                        10 8
      West                              East
      Lead 6                           A 7 5
                        South
```

South is playing a no-trump contract.

East wins the lead with the Ace, South playing the 2. If East needs to determine whether West has a five-card or only a four-card suit, he uses the rule of fourteen as follows: the card led, the 6, tentatively assumed to be from a five-card suit, is subtracted from 10, which gives a result of four cards higher than the 6. Four higher cards are visible in dummy's and East's hands, which means in turn that South cannot have any card higher than the 6. However, this cannot be true, since West, if holding K Q J 9 6, would have made a conventional sequence lead. Consequently, West can only have a four-card suit.

The rule of fourteen can also be used to locate the honour cards.

```
                        North
                        Q 9 5 2
      West                              East
      Lead 7                           A J 8 4
                        South
```

South is playing a suit contract. West leads the 7 of a side suit in which South may be assumed to hold at most a doubleton, but not a void. Using the rule of fourteen East subtracts 7 from 12 (three or four-card suit), which makes five higher cards, equal to the higher cards in dummy's and East's hands. Consequently South cannot head the 7, and if dummy ducks, East can do the same.

So much for a brief introduction to the distributional signal, so far as its basic principles and main rules are concerned. We must now discuss various details which are not the same for leads, plays, or discards. From now on we shall be talking about:

> Leads that give the count
> Signals that give the count.

LEADS THAT GIVE THE COUNT

The opening lead initiates the teamwork between the defenders. It is very important at this stage to convey information about length.

Short suits

The rules for a doubleton lead and for a lead from three cards should be studied together. The difference of one card is vital in defensive play. It is essential to indicate the difference by playing high-low with a doubleton, low-high with a three-card suit.

                     North
                     J 9 2
West   East
(1) 6 3   A K 10 8 5 4
(2) 7 6 3
                     South
                     (1) Q 7
                     (2) Q

South is playing a trump contract.

In Alternative 1 West leads the 6. East can immediately read this card as a doubleton, whether South plays the 7 or the Queen. This enables East to cash his two honours and play a third round to kill dummy's chance of winning a trick with the Jack.

In Alternative 2 West leads the 3, East reading it as a three-card suit. East now has to switch to another suit, otherwise dummy's Jack will make a trick. A short-suit lead that fails to distinguish a doubleton from a three-card suit would have presented East with a problem, and he would have to guess whether South – playing the Queen in both cases – held another card.

```
                North
                8 7 4
West                            East
(1) 6 3                         K Q 10 9 2
(2) 6 5 3
                South
                (1) A J 5
                (2) A J
```

South is playing a no-trump contract, West leading the suit bid by East.

In Alternative 1 West leads the 6 and East reads this as a doubleton. He may now insert the 9, forcing South to take the first trick with the Jack. The result of this play is that communication still exists between East and West. This would have been lost if East had played the Queen on the lead, South ducking.

In Alternative 2 West leads the 3, and East reads this as indicating a three-card suit. In this case the right play is the Queen, as South can only have two cards in the suit. If East has to lead the suit on the next round, he will cash the King, knowing that either the Jack will fall from South or that West will unblock if he began with J x x.

Long Suits

The commonest lead when playing against a no-trump contract is from a long suit, either a four-card suit or a five-card suit. In most cases the conventional lead will distinguish between the two possibilities.

	North	
	10 8	
West		East
(1) K 9 5 4		A 7 6
(2) K 9 5 4 3		
	South	
	(1) Q J 3 2	
	(2) Q J 2	

South is playing a no-trump contract.

In Alternative 1 West leads the 5, his next lowest, indicating a four-card suit, and East plays the Ace. To discover whether West has a four-card suit or a much more interesting five-card suit, East uses the rule of fourteen, tentatively assuming that West has a five-card suit. 5 from 10 = 5 and five higher cards are visible, so none are left for South. However, this possibility can be excluded, as West would not have led the 5 from K Q J 9 5. Consequently both West and South have a four-card suit, which means that there is no long-card trick to be established. This knowledge enables East to judge the best line of defence.

In Alternative 2 West leads the 3, the lowest, indicating a five-card suit. East returns the 7, indicating that he has two cards left, and West allows South to hold the second trick, preparatory to cashing three more tricks later on.

As any player knows from experience, the difference between a five-card suit and a four-card suit is critical. Equally, it is very useful to be able to appraise a six-card suit.

North
QJ

West   East
Lead 5   A 9 6

South

South is playing a no-trump contract.

Let us assume that East, owing to the bidding, can exclude the possibility of South holding as many as four cards in the suit. He takes the Ace, and when South plays the 2 East uses the rule of fourteen to assess the strength of the suit in West's hand. If West has a five-card suit South cannot have any card higher than the 5; in this case there are five top tricks to be made. If West has a six-card suit, South being assumed to have the King, there are still five tricks to be made if the suit is returned, since dummy's and declarer's honour cards will fall in the second round.

Against trump contracts a four-card suit is more likely to develop tricks than a five-card suit.

North
A 9 8

West   East
(1) Q 10 5 3   K 7 6
(2) Q 10 5 3 2

South
(1) J 4 2
(2) J 4

South is playing a trump contract.

In Alternative 1 West leads the 5, his next lowest, and East wins with the King. Thanks to the lead he knows that West has four cards, and returning the suit may establish an extra trick.

In Alternative 2 West leads the 2. If dummy plays low and East wins with the King, he knows that no further top tricks can be won in this suit. It may still be wise to return the suit to initiate a forcing game. Once again, the knowledge of a five-card suit may be important.

Variations

Some players, when leading from a three-card suit, prefer the lowest from three to an honour, the 5 from Q 6 5, but the middle card from three small, the 6 from 7 6 2. They follow the 6 with the 7 – the method known as MUD (middle, up, down).

This system is not recommended. In many cases the MUD lead will leave partner guessing about length. Here is an example against a no-trump contract:

	North	
	J 9 8 4	
West		East
(1) 6 5 3		A K 10 7
(2) 5 3		
	South	
	(1) Q 2	
	(2) Q 6 2	

West, having no better suit to lead, starts off with the 5 in both alternatives, if playing MUD. Dummy plays the 8, East the King, and South the 2. How is it possible for East to judge whether West has a doubleton or a three-card suit? The answer is: he cannot – he has to guess. In Alternative 1 the return of the 7 will open the way for two more tricks when West next has the lead. In Alternative 2 East will have to turn to another suit if he is not to lose a trick as well as a tempo.

Occasionally the MUD lead will be helpful, but generally speaking it is more important to give information about length than strength.

From a worthless four-card suit the third lowest, instead of the next lowest, may be led. The principle is 'second from the top of bad suits', the 7 from 8 7 4 2.

The same principle applies to five-card suits. You have to lead against 3NT from:

♠ J 3
♡ 9 7 6 4 2
◇ A Q J 7
♣ J 2

The best chance of defeating the contract seems to lie in diamonds, where South probably holds the King. A conventional lead of ♡ 2 would be ill-judged. The best tactical lead is ♡ 7. East will probably be able to read this lead and switch to diamonds at the first opportunity.

The new third hand rule

Standard practice for third hand is to play high in response to partner's lead of a small card. This will generally be the correct play, but not invariably. The conventional leads we have described create a new rule for third hand in certain circumstances.

On a long-suit lead against a no-trump contract third hand should play high except in the following case:

If dummy and third hand hold only spot cards in the suit, and the sum of leader's, dummy's and third hand's cards makes eleven, third hand should play his lowest card.

The reason for this rule is as follows:

When leading a low card the leader cannot hold A Q J x or K Q J x, because with these combinations he would have led an honour. (Theoretically, the leader may hold either A K Q x x or A K J x x and choose to lead a low card, but in that case the card played by third hand will be irrelevant.)

Consequently, if leader, dummy, and third hand hold a total of eleven cards in the suit, the two remaining cards in declarer's hand will normally be two honour cards. When third hand plays his lowest card and declarer wins with an honour the leader will know the exact distribution of the suit.

When the lead indicates a *six-card suit*, third hand must play his lowest card if dummy and third hand hold a sum total of *five spot cards*.

<pre>
                    North
                    9 7
West   East
A J 8 5 4 2   10 6 3
                    South
                    K Q
</pre>

South is playing a no-trump contract.

West leads the 5, his third lowest. Provided East calculates that South cannot have as many as four cards in the suit, he follows the new third hand rule, playing the 3, his lowest. South is forced to play an honour, and West knows that he can lay down the Ace as soon as he obtains the lead.

The theoretical possibility of a five-card suit does not affect the rule because:

If the lead of the 5 is from a five-card suit, it should be the lowest card. In that case the leader must hold one of the following combinations: A K Q 8 5 or A K J 8 5. If so, his four tricks are already established whatever cards are played by East and South.

Conclusion: when dummy and third hand hold a total of five spot cards, third hand must play his lowest card if declarer can reasonably be assumed to have at most three cards in the suit.

When the lead indicates a *five-card suit* third hand should play his lowest card if dummy and third hand hold a total of *six spot cards.*

<pre>
                    North
                    9 7 4
West   East
A Q 8 5 2   10 6 3
                    South
                    K J
</pre>

South is playing a no-trump contract.

West leads the 2, indicating a five-card suit. East seeing six spot cards plays the 3. When South is forced to win with an honour West knows the exact distribution.

When the lead indicates a *four-card suit* third hand should play his lowest card if dummy and third hand hold a total of *seven spot cards*.

North
9 7 4

West
A J 5 2

East
10 8 6 3

South
K Q

South is playing a no-trump contract.

West leads the 5 indicating a four-card suit. East plays the 3, and when South wins with an honour West has all the information he requires.

The new third hand rule is effective in a great many situations where the standard rule 'play high for partner' would leave the leader guessing. When the lead is from weaker holdings than those shown above the third hand rule may still provide indications. For example:

North
9 6 5

West
K J 8 7 3

East
10 4 2

South
A Q

South is playing a no-trump contract.

West leads the 3, East plays the 2, and South is forced to win with the Queen. West now possesses the important information that East holds three cards in the suit. This tells West that the suit is worth continuing even when he has no other entry.

The new third hand rule provides equally important negative indications.

<pre>
                          North
                          9 6 5

West   East
A Q 8 7 3   10 2

                          South
                          K J 4
</pre>

South is playing a no-trump contract.

West leads the 3, indicating a five-card suit. Here dummy and third hand hold a total of five spot cards between them. The third hand rule is put into effect only when six spot cards are visible, so here East has to play the 10, which is won by South's Jack. In this case West knows that South holds K J x, because if East had held 10 4 2 and South K J, East would have played the 2 in accordance with the third hand rule.

The opening leader should always trust his partner to follow the third hand rule. Here is an example from play:

<pre>
                          North
                          ♠ 9 7 6
                          ♡ 10 7 4
                          ◇ Q J 10 8
                          ♣ J 6 3

West   East
♠ A J 8 4 2   ♠ 10 5 3
♡ A 8 6   ♡ 9 5 2
◇ 5 2   ◇ K 7 6 4
♣ 10 9 4   ♣ 8 5 2

                          South
                          ♠ K Q
                          ♡ K Q J 3
                          ◇ A 9 3
                          ♣ A K Q 7
</pre>

<pre>
        South   North
        2 ♣   2 ◇
        2NT   3NT
</pre>

The ♠ 2 is led.

East interprets the lead as indicating a five-card suit, which means the conditions necessary for the use of the third hand rule are present (5 + 6 = 11). East plays the 3 and as South has to drop the Queen the situation is completely clear to West. He therefore takes the Ace of hearts as soon as this suit is played and lays down the Ace of spades.

Compare this with a fourth-best lead of ♠ 4 and the routine 10 from East. South will win and play a high honour in hearts. West will probably duck to prevent ♡ 10 from affording an entry. South will hastily cross to ♣ J, take the diamond finesse, and run nine tricks.

SIGNALS THAT GIVE THE COUNT

We turn now to signals made not on the lead but in the course of play.

Short suits

We follow standard procedure by playing high-low from a doubleton, low-high from three cards.

	North	
	Q 9 6	
West		**East**
A K 10 5 2		(1) 8 3
		(2) 8 7 3
	South	
	(1) J 7 4	
	(2) J 4	

South is playing a trump contract.

West leads an honour. In Alternative 1 East plays the 8 (high-low), indicating a doubleton, and West knows he can give partner a ruff. In Alternative 2 East plays the three (low-high), indicating a three-card suit. Whether South plays the 4 or the Jack, West knows that both his honours will stand up, but also that dummy's Queen will then provide South with a discard.

Against no-trump contracts a three-card suit is normally a better holding for third hand than a doubleton.

North
8 5 2

West
K Q J 9

East
(1) 7 3
(2) 7 6 3

South
(1) A 10 6 4
(2) A 10 4

South is playing a no-trump contract.

West, leading an honour, makes the first trick. In Alternative 1 East plays the 7 indicating a doubleton. West knows at once what to do. To win three tricks, he must switch to another suit since to continue the sequence lead will destroy communication with East. If three tricks are to be made, East must have an entry to play through South and West must have an entry to cash his established tricks later on.

In Alternative 2 East plays the 3, indicating a three-card suit, and West knows that he can establish the suit by continuing it.

Long Suits

When signalling long suits it is again very important to distinguish between the two suit-lengths adjacent to one another, especially four and five-card suits.

                    North
                    Q 8 5
West   East
A K 10 7   (1) J 9 4 3
                                        (2) J 9 6 4 3

                    South
                    (1) 6 2
                    (2) 2

South plays a trump contract.

West leads an honour. In Alternative 1 East plays the 4, indicating a four-card suit (it cannot be a five-card suit) and West now knows that both his honours will stand up. In Alternative 2 East plays the 3, indicating a five-card (or a three-card) suit. As a rule, the bidding will indicate which is the more likely.

Against no-trump contracts a five-card suit is likely to be of more assistance to partner.

                    North
                    K Q
West   East
J 9 5 2   (1) 10 8 7 3
                                        (2) 10 8 7 6 3

                    South
                    (1) A 6 4
                    (2) A 4

West leads the 5. In Alternative 1 East plays the 7, the next lowest, excluding a five-card suit. This tells West that his opponents have three winning cards in the suit and he will have to look for a better attack when next in the lead.

In Alternative 2 East plays the 3, indicating a five-card suit which West will probably be able to read correctly in the light of the bidding. He will obviously continue with this suit, establishing three tricks.

Variations

When signalling and reading signals, the defenders should be aware of the possibility of declarer false-carding. However, this can effectively be prevented when signalling a four-card suit by playing the *third lowest* instead of the next lowest. When the third lowest is played, the opener will realise that his partner does not hold five cards or three.

                          North
                          Q 9 6 2
        West   East
        A K 10 8   (1) 7 5 4 3
                                            (2) 7 5 4
                          South
                          (1) J
                          (2) J 3

South is playing a suit contract.

West leads an honour. In Alternative 1 East should play the 5, the third lowest, because if he plays the 4 and South plays the Jack, West will not be able to figure out whether East or South holds the 3. If East plays the 5, however, West will have an exact count: East cannot hold 7 5, as he would then have had to play the 7. Nor can he have 7 5 x as he would then play his lowest card, which cannot be the 5. Consequently, East must have played the 5 from 7 5 4 3, using the third-lowest signal.

In Alternative 2 East plays the 4, whereupon South, adopting false-carding tactics, plays the Jack and West now has to puzzle out whether the Jack is a singleton. Since East would have used the third lowest to signal a four-card suit, West concludes that the play of the 4 denies a four-card suit. Consequently, South must hold the 3.

A NEW TRUMP SIGNAL

The traditional trump echo, high-low from an odd number, has limited value. An alternative scheme opens up entirely new perspectives for precision defence against trump contracts.

The principle

The new trump signal is based on the same principle that applies to the distribution signal, viz. the 'two-card difference' principle.

A hand consisting of 13 cards is bound to contain three suits with an odd number, one with an even number, or vice versa. We call this the hand's *distribution pattern*.

For example, a 4 – 3 – 3 – 3 hand has a distribution pattern of one suit with an even number of cards and three suits with an odd number, whereas a 4 – 4 – 3 – 2 type has one suit with an odd number of cards and three suits with an even number. If we include voids, a hand will always contain distribution types in a proportion of 1:3.

This simple fact provides the basis for the new trump signal which instead of marking trump length indicates the hand's distribution pattern.

Signalling rule

The trump signal indicates the distribution type in this manner:

> High-low shows that the hand is one even, three odd.
> Low-high shows that the hand is one odd, three even.

On the basis of this simple signal partner will be in a position to interpret the distribution type held in both concealed hands as soon as he can identify the *one* suit that is even or the *one* suit that is odd.

Interpreting the trump signal

Sometimes, obviously, the need to play a winning or constructive card on the first round of the trump suit will prevent immediate use of the trump signal. Such situations are easy to read.

When the player's length in the trump suit is known and this corresponds to the 'one-odd' or 'one-even', his distribution pattern can be gauged at once.

Let us now consider a few examples of the use of the new trump signal, and the possibilities it offers defence:

<pre>
                    ♠ Q 10 9 4
                    ♡ A 9 2
                    ◊ 8 5 3
                    ♣ Q J 7
    West   East
    ♠ 8 2   ♠ A 6 3
    ♡ K 10 4   ♡ Q 7 5 3
    ◊ Q J 10 7 6   ◊ 9 4 2
    ♣ K 8 2   ♣ 6 4 3
                    South
                    ♠ K J 7 5
                    ♡ J 8 6
                    ◊ A K
                    ♣ A 10 9 5

            South   North
            1NT   2 ♣
            2 ♠   4 ♠
</pre>

West leads from his sequence in diamonds.

South wins with the King and plays the ♠ K, which is allowed to hold. He continues with a small spade and East now wins with the Ace. West's trump signal, playing trumps in the order 8 2, has now provided East with a full picture of the distribution type in all suits:

In spades, the trump suit, West must hold a doubleton. Furthermore, with West marking high-low and in this way indicating that he has one suit with an even number of cards – which must be trumps – he is bound to have an odd number of cards in the three side suits.

In hearts, West must hold three cards, because South, in view of his no-trump opening, cannot be 5-4 in the majors.

Consequently South, too, holds three hearts.

In diamonds and clubs, West must be 5-3 or 3-5, which means that South is either 2-4 or 4-2 in these suits.

East can now work out a successful way of beating the contract on the basis of the following reasoning: *if South holds four clubs and consequently two diamonds*, the fourth club will provide a discard in dummy. There would be no point in discarding a diamond, since South himself in this case only holds two cards in the suit. On the other hand, dummy can get rid of a possible loser in hearts where South likewise can be shown to possess three cards. For this reason the correct procedure must be to attack immediately in hearts. *If South held two clubs and consequently four diamonds* again it would be essential to attack hearts.

Let us, however, imagine an alternative distribution which is equally consistent with South's bidding:

North
♠ Q 10 9 4
♡ A 9 2
◊ 8 5 3
♣ Q J 7

West
♠ 8 2
♡ J 8 4
◊ Q J 10 7
♣ A 10 8 2

East
♠ A 6 3
♡ Q 7 5 3
◊ 9 4 2
♣ 6 4 3

South
♠ K J 7 5
♡ K 10 6
◊ A K 6
♣ K 9 5

With this distribution South will make his contract if East switches to hearts when he obtains the lead with the Ace of spades, as he will now win three tricks in hearts, as opposed to two if he has to play the suit himself. This time East must return his partner's diamond lead.

However, the trump signal solves this problem: West now plays low-high in trumps, indicating one suit with an odd number of cards. As he holds a doubleton in trumps, he must consequently hold an odd number of one of the side-suits. If this is hearts, it is bound to be a three-card suit and he will hold four cards in both diamonds and clubs. This in turn means that South's distribution must be $4 - 3 - 3 - 3$ and he has no possibility of obtaining a discard. If on the other hand West has an odd number of cards in diamonds or clubs, he must have an even number of hearts and again the heart lead would achieve nothing. After a diamond return South has to play hearts himself and inevitably goes down. (Note that South can win his contract if East returns a club, exposing his partner to an end-play).

The next example illustrates a combination of lead and trump signals which make it possible to analyse the distribution of all suits in time.

North
♠ J 10
♡ A J 8
◇ A 7 5
♣ K 10 7 6 4

West
♠ 7 6 2
♡ Q 6 5 4 2
◇ Q J 3
♣ 9 2

East
♠ A 4
♡ K 9 7 3
◇ 10 9 8 4
♣ A J 8

South
♠ K Q 9 8 5 3
♡ 10
◇ K 6 2
♣ Q 5 3

North	South
1 ♣	1 ♠
1 NT	3 ♠
4 ♠	

The ♣ 9 is led.

The lead is covered by the 10, Jack and Queen. South continues with a small spade, West plays the 6 and dummy's 10 holds the trick. East wins the next round, West playing the 2. Thanks to the combination of lead and trump signal, East acquires the following information: West has indicated that he holds one suit with an even number of cards, and this suit is identified by the lead of ♣ 9. Consequently, West must have three spades and also odd holdings in hearts and diamonds. As yet, East has no idea whether West holds five hearts and three diamonds or vice versa, but what he does know is that if West has three diamonds, so has South. In that case diamonds must be attacked immediately as otherwise South might be able to get rid of a diamond loser on dummy's fourth club. For this reason, East switches to diamonds and South wins with the King. He draws West's last trump and then leads a club, losing to the 8. The question now is: does South hold a King singleton in diamonds and three hearts, or does he have three to the King in diamonds and a singleton heart? The answer is provided by West's play of ◊ 3. This means that he cannot hold five diamonds, because in that event he would have indicated a five-card suit by playing the 2. Consequently, West and South must both hold three diamonds, and East returns diamonds, establishing a diamond trick for West, while East still possesses the master card in clubs. In this way the contract is defeated.

In this example, too, we shall see an alternative distribution pattern, just as probable on the bidding:

                        South
                        ♠ J 10
                        ♡ A J 8
                        ◊ A 7 5
                        ♣ K 10 7 6 4

West   East
♠ 7 6 2   ♠ A 4
♡ Q 6 4 2   ♡ K 9 7 3
◊ Q J 3 2   ◊ 10 9 8 4
♣ 9 2   ♣ A J 8

                        South
                        ♠ K Q 9 8 5 3
                        ♡ 10 5
                        ◊ K 6
                        ♣ Q 5 3

The ♣ 9 is led.

The first three tricks are played as in the previous example, but with one important difference, viz. that West now plays trumps in the sequence 2 – 6, indicating one suit with an odd number of cards. As this can be identified as the trump suit, since South obviously holds a six-card suit in trumps, West must have an even number of cards in the three side-suits. He has already indicated a doubleton in clubs by his lead, and it is highly probable that he therefore holds four cards in both diamonds and hearts. This means that South has the following distribution: six spades – two hearts – two diamonds – three clubs. East now realises there is a possibility of defeating the contract with one trump trick, two club tricks, and one trick in hearts or diamonds. The important thing is to play the suits in the right order. First, he switches to diamonds in the hope of establishing a diamond trick in West's hand. South, however, wins with the King, extracts West's last trump, and plays clubs, losing to the 8. The situation is now quite clear to East: South has no diamond losers, but he is in a position to establish dummy's fourth club, on which he can then discard a losing heart in his own hand. Consequently, the only chance of defeating the contract is to find West with the

Queen of hearts. East therefore switches to a heart and defeats the contract.

The next example shows how the new trump signal works in a ruffing situation:

```
                    North
                    ♠ Q 8 7
                    ♡ A J 9 8
                    ◊ Q 10 9 4
                    ♣ K Q

West                                   East
♠ 6 4 2                                ♠ A 5
♡ 3                                    ♡ Q 10 7 5 2
◊ 8 7 5 3                              ◊ K 6 2
♣ J 8 6 5 3                            ♣ A 9 4

                    South
                    ♠ K J 10 9 3
                    ♡ K 6 4
                    ◊ A J
                    ♣ 10 7 2
```

North	South
1 ♡	1 ♠
2 ♠	4 ♠

West leads the ♡ 3.

The first trick goes to South's King. He continues with the ♠ J. West plays the ♠ 4 and East the Ace. East interprets the opening lead as a singleton and returns the ♡ 2 in order to show that he would like clubs returned after West's ruff. West ruffs with the ♠ 2 and switches to the ♣ 3. East is now in a position to assess the possibilities open to the defence on the basis of the following information:

West has shown that he is one even, three odd, by playing trumps in the sequence 4 – 2. Can he hold a doubleton in trumps? In that event he has an odd number of cards in all side suits, and this in turn would mean that he was 5 – 5 in the minors. If West in fact holds five diamonds the contract cannot be defeated, so East must place West with three trumps and play for another heart ruff.

The hand might alternatively have been:

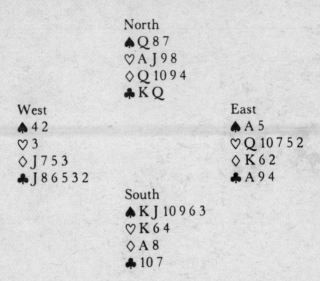

North
♠ Q 8 7
♡ A J 9 8
◇ Q 10 9 4
♣ K Q

West
♠ 4 2
♡ 3
◇ J 7 5 3
♣ J 8 6 5 3 2

East
♠ A 5
♡ Q 10 7 5 2
◇ K 6 2
♣ A 9 4

South
♠ K J 10 9 6 3
♡ K 6 4
◇ A 8
♣ 10 7

The first tricks proceed as in the previous example except that West indicates one odd, three even, by playing trumps in the sequence 2 – 4. As the suit with the odd number of cards is identified as the singleton in hearts, West must have an even number of spades, diamonds, and clubs. South's game bid after North's single raise obviously means that South holds six cards – not four cards – in spades, and consequently West's even number of spades must constitute a doubleton. This makes it clear that West cannot ruff again. East exists safely in clubs and South must eventually concede a trick in diamonds.

HAND-PATTERN SIGNAL AT NO-TRUMPS

Can the 'Trump Signal' be used at no-trumps? It can, indeed! The scheme below was formulated after this book was written and was first described in *Bridge i Norge*, early in 1979. The article reads as follows:

Some months ago I became the victim of wrong-guessing. This was the hand, which occurred in a pairs tournament:

```
                    North
                    ♠ A K J 8
                    ♡ Q J 10
                    ◇ A 5
                    ♣ Q J 4 2
West                                East
♠ 7 5                               ♠ 6 4 3 2
♡ K 9 7 4                           ♡ 8 6 5
◇ J 9 3 2                           ◇ 8 7 6
♣ 10 8 3                            ♣ K 9 6
                    South
                    ♠ Q 10 9
                    ♡ A 3 2
                    ◇ K Q 10 4
                    ♣ A 7 5
```

        South   North
        1NT (15-17) 6NT

Sitting West, I led the ♠ 7, which was won in dummy. The heart finesse lost to my king and I returned the ♠ 5. Declarer now took his two tricks in hearts and ran the spade suit. On the last round declarer discarded the ♣ 5, leaving me guessing whether to discard a club or a diamond. I made the wrong guess, discarding a diamond, and the contract was made.

How on earth could I know that East and South did not hold these hands:

North

West   East
                                                  ♠ 6 4 3 2
                                                  ♡ 8 6 5
                                                  ◇ x x x x
                                                  ♣ K x

South
♠ Q 10 9
♡ A 3 2
◇ K Q 10
♣ A x x 5

A study of the problem gave an interesting answer. If the principles of the new trump signal were used also against no-trump contracts, this should be a solution. All that was needed was to identify a signalling suit instead of the trump suit. Here is my suggestion:

The signalling suit should be the first suit bid and supported by the opponents (declarer and dummy), and if no suit has been bid and supported, the signalling suit should be the first suit initially led by declarer or dummy.

Now back to the example above. According to the rules, hearts in this case is defined to be the signalling suit, as no suit has been bid and supported and hearts is the first suit initially led by dummy (or declarer). So, on the heart lead, East starts signalling the distribution pattern, one suit even, three odd, by playing the 6 followed by the 5. As East's one even suit is known to be spades, West knows that East is 4 – 3 – 3 – 3. This marks South with 3 – 3 – 4 – 3. West can now safely discard a club and the contract will be defeated.

Another example:

```
                    North
                    ♠ 10 8 3
                    ♡ 9 7 5 3
                    ◊ K Q 10 2
                    ♣ K 2
        West                        East
        ♠ J 6                       ♠ Q 9 7 5
        ♡ A Q J 8                   ♡ 6 4 2
        ◊ 8 6 3                     ◊ 7 5
        ♣ Q 7 6 4                   ♣ J 9 8 5
                    South
                    ♠ A K 4 2
                    ♡ K 10
                    ◊ A J 9 4
                    ♣ A 10 3
```

South	North
1 ◊	2 ◊
3NT	

West chooses a passive lead in diamonds. As the diamond suit has been bid and supported, this suit is defined as the signalling suit. West therefore leads the ◊ 3 to show the distribution pattern: one suit odd, three even. The trick is taken by dummy and a heart is played to declarer's king. West wins with the ace and returns the ◊ 6. Declarer plays another round of hearts, taken by West, who again exits in diamonds. After a fourth round of diamonds dummy has the lead in this position:

North
♠ 10 8 3
♡ 9 7
◊ K
♣ K 2

West
♠ J 6
♡ Q 8
◊ –
♣ Q 7 6 4

East
♠ Q 9 7 5
♡ –
◊ –
♣ J 9 8 5

South
♠ A K 4 2
♡ –
◊ J
♣ A 10 3

How should East know whether to discard a spade or a club?

The hand-pattern signal solves the problem. West has signalled one suit odd, three even, and as the one odd suit is known to be diamonds he must be 2 – 4 – 3 – 4, which leaves South with 4 – 2 – 4 – 3. Consequently, East can safely discard a club.

POSITIVE AND NEGATIVE SIGNALS

As we stated in our preamble we also provide a scheme for signalling strength or weakness in special circumstances. We prefer to use the terms *positive* and *negative* signals, instead of the traditional terms, encouraging and discouraging. We employ such signals only to reply to a specific question. For example, when the lead is from A K x against a trump contract the leader is interested to know whether partner holds the Queen but not the Jack. On a conventional lead from K Q x the leader is looking for the Jack or, if possible, the Ace.

One lead must be considered separately: the lead of the Ace. In spite of the fact that an Ace lead has its place in the scheme of sequence leads, this card may also be led when on the lookout for quick tricks. When an Ace lead of this kind is not the opening lead, but a subsequent one, the situation will obviously make it clear to partner that the intention is to cash the quick tricks immediately. The Ace will call for a positive or a negative signal in that particular suit.

Positive or negative signals to show strength or weakness are used:

Generally:

On Ace leads in situations where the defenders are obviously compelled to make their quick tricks immediately.

Particularly:

On honour leads, in accordance with the rules for signalling on sequence leads (set out in detail under sequence technique).

Thus we do not recommend the use of signals to show strength or weakness on partner's spot card lead, nor when discarding. In such cases we prefer counting signals that provide absolute information independent of partner's holding in the suit. In general, we rely on the simple method of discarding from the weaker suit to indicate strength in another suit. At times, also, we may invoke suit-preference signals.

Signalling method

In accordance with the general principle that a signal should be easy for partner to read, we use the two-card difference principle.

A positive signal is given by playing the *lowest* card in the suit.

A negative signal is given by playing the *third-lowest* card in the suit, but the *next lowest* if the third-lowest is an *active* card.

Clearly it is advantageous to be able to signal with the low card from a combination such as K J 2 or Q 10 2. Another virtue is that such signals give partner the best chance to read the position quickly, whether the declarer is using deceptive cards or not.

North
9 8

West
(1) K Q 10 7
(2) K Q 10 5

East
(1) 5 4 3
(2) J 4 3

South
(1) A J 6 2
(2) A 7 6 2

Against a no-trump contract West leads the King, which is assumed to be a conventional lead from K Q 10 x. The Jack is now the critical card.

In Alternative 1 East plays the 5 – his third lowest. Whether South takes the trick with the Ace or holds up, West can interpret the signal as negative, because there are still two lower outstanding cards.

In Alternative 2 East plays the 3 – his lowest – indicating a positive signal. Whether South plays the 2 or 6, West can interpret the signal as positive, because a negative signal would involve playing the third lowest and, of course, the 3 cannot be the third lowest.

However, cases may arise where a negative signal will have to be given by playing the next lowest card, because the third lowest is an active card. This may depend on the cards held by dummy.

North
8 4

West
K Q 10 5

East
9 7 2

South
A J 6 3

Against a no-trump contract West leads the King. If East plays the 9 South can ensure a double stop by winning with the Ace. The 9 may be useful later, so East should play the 7.

General recommendation for reading positive or negative signals:

The signalling card should be read as a positive signal when the card is the lowest of the outstanding cards.

The signalling card should be read as a negative signal when the card is the third lowest (or higher) of the outstanding cards.

When the card is the next lowest of the outstanding cards, the leader must examine the overall situation.

SUIT PREFERENCE SIGNAL

The suit preference signal should be used in situations where the defender in the lead is obviously compelled to switch to a suit other than the one played and needs guidance from his partner. This is the system:

When partner plays an unusually high card he wants a switch to the higher-ranking of the alternative suits.

When partner plays a low card he wants a switch to the lower suit.

The suit preference signal is effective in situations such as the following:

1. Against trump contracts when the leader, after winning the first trick, obviously has to switch to another suit owing to dummy's hand, e.g. when dummy holds a singleton in the suit played.

2. Against trump contracts when a defender, giving partner a ruff, wants a particular suit to be returned. This situation may arise either after an opening lead, where the leader is in a position to give partner a ruff, or after an opening short suit lead from partner which results in a similar situation.

	North	
	Q 8 4	
West		East
A K 7 5 3		9 2
	South	
	J 10 6	

South is playing a suit contract.

West takes the first two tricks with A K, and when East plays high-low, the coast is clear for a ruffing trick. This is a suit preference situation, where West, in playing the third round, may indicate the suit he would like in return. The 7 would indicate that he wanted the higher-ranking suit; the 3 would suggest that he wanted the lower suit. This, of course, is already standard practice.

3. Against no-trump contracts, a defender gives a suit preference signal when establishing his long suit.

North
9 8 5

West
K 10 7 6 4

East
A 3

South
Q J 2

South is playing a no-trump contract.

West leads the 4. East takes the Ace and returns the 3, West winning with the King. West's next lead will be a suit preference signal. He will lead the 10 if he wants the higher and the 6 if he wants the lowers suit.

Note that the suit preference signal in this situation would not always be clear after a standard lead of the fourth-highest. The lead of the 10 on the third round might be necessary to pin dummy's 9, if the leader held K 10 7 6 alone. This doubt does not arise in our scheme, because the lead of the 4 shows the five-card suit.

North
8 5

West
K 10 7 4 2

East
Q J 3

South
A 9 6

South is playing a no-trump contract.

West lead the 2, East taking the first two tricks with the Jack and the Queen. On the third round West, with K 10 7 remaining, has an obvious opportunity for a suit preference signal.

A POSITIVE OR NEGATIVE SIGNAL FOLLOWED BY A LENGTH SIGNAL

A positive or negative or even a suit preference signal may be followed on the next round by a signal indicating length. This form of combined signalling is of particular interest when the first signal is a negative one. The partner may nevertheless have sufficient length to make a continuation desirable.

                    North
                    10 9
West   East
A K Q 6   (1) 7 5 4 3
                                        (2) 8 7 3
                    South
                    (1) J 8 2
                    (2) J 5 4 2

South is playing a no-trump contract.

When West starts off with two honour cards East may use combined signalling in the following way:

In Alternative 1 he plays the 5, his third lowest, on the first lead, as a negative signal. However on the second round he plays the 3, a delayed counting signal indicating that he has an odd number left (7 4 3).

In Alternative 2 East plays the 8, his third lowest, on the first lead, a negative signal. On the second he plays the 7, a delayed counting signal indicating that he has an even number left (7 3).

OCCASIONS WHEN A ROUTINE SIGNAL MAY BE INADVISABLE

A player must not be a slave to his signalling system. Let us now consider for a moment a few special occasions when it may be advisable to refrain from signalling.

Active cards

Whether a card is active or not will depend on the particular situation. In some cases it will be obvious when a card is active; in others, a certain degree of doubt may exist.

1.

	North K 10 9 4	
West J 7		East Q 5 3
	South A 8 6 2	

2.

	North K J 9 4	
West 10 7		East Q 5 3
	South A 8 6 2	

South plays the 2 from his own hand. In Alternative 1 it is obvious that West must play the 7 and not the Jack. In Alternative 2 the play of the 10 might cause declarer to take a backward finesse against the Queen.

Often a card will be active in another sense:

North
762

West   East
KJ9   1053

South
AQ8

South, playing a suit contract, has carried out the steps preparatory to a throw-in and plays the suit from dummy. Here the 10 is an active card, which should be used as the counter to upset declarer's plan. Similarly, if East had to lead, the 10 would be the correct card.

Valuable card combinations

The opening lead from a combination such as KJ92 (generally undesirable, of course) presents a problem: which card should be led?

General recommendation:

If there is nothing to indicate how the suit will break, the best plan is to follow the rule and lead the 9. Occasionally you will be sacrificing a valuable card, but on the other hand you may be unblocking in a situation such as this:

North
63

West   East
KJ92   Q8754

South
A10

If there are indications that the suit is likely to break 4 – 4 – 3 – 2, with one of the opponents holding a four-card length, and a lead of this suit seems to offer the best prospects, then the 9 should be led if the four-card length is expected to be in dummy. This lead will prove the best if the suit breaks as follows:

                              North
                              A 10 5 3

West   East
K J 9 2   Q 6 4

                              South
                              8 7

                              North
                              10 6 5 3

West   East
K J 9 2   Q 7 4

                              South
                              A 8

If, however, the four-card suit is expected to be in declarer's hand, it is better to lead the lowest card, because the distribution may well be such as this:

                              North
                              8 7

West   East
K J 9 2   Q 6 4

                              South
                              A 10 5 3

                              North
                              10 8

West   East
K J 9 2   Q 6 4

                              South
                              A 7 5 3

Tactical considerations

Obviously there are occasions when to give the standard signal would be more helpful to the declarer than to partner. It cannot be sensible to assist the declarer in a situation like this:

North
Q 10 7 5

West   East
J 9 4 3   6 2

South
A K 8

South plays the Ace and King and notes the order in which defenders play their cards. If both West and East play high-low he will infer that the suit is breaking 4 – 2. The optimum strategy in situations of this kind is highly complicated. It depends on psychological considerations such as which defender, if either, is likely to play an irregular card. It is best (as in many similar situations) to vary tactics.

TECHNIQUE FOR LEADS FROM A SEQUENCE

Definitions

Solid sequence   – At least three cards in a sequence e.g.
                         A K Q – K Q J – Q J 10 – J 10 9

Incomplete sequence   – At least three cards with a break before the lowest e.g.
                         A K J – K Q 10 – Q J 9 – J 10 8

Intermediate sequence – At least three cards with a break between the first and second e.g.
                         A Q J – K J 10 – A 10 9 – Q 10 9

Partial sequence   – Two consecutive cards e.g.
                         A K x – K Q x – Q J x – J 10 x

A satisfactory system of sequence leads has two aims: to indicate the nature of the sequence and to enable the partner to indicate the nature of his support.

SEQUENCE LEADS AT NO-TRUMPS

Standard leads have many unsatisfactory areas, as all experienced players are aware. This is true whether you play Roman leads or the more traditional style.

We have constructed a new table for sequence leads against no-trump contracts, based on the following principles:

Sequence leads should so far as possible be unambiguous, indicating whether the leader holds a perfect sequence or an incomplete sequence or a partial sequence.

Sequence leads which are inevitably ambiguous, owing to the many variations involved, should so far as possible give partner the best chance to distinguish between one type and another.

TABLE FOR OPENING LEADS AT NO-TRUMPS

Holding in suit	Lead	Reading
A K (x –)	Ace	Partial sequence without other honours in the suit.
A K J (x –) K Q 10 (x –)	King	Incomplete sequence lacking the Queen or the Jack.
A K Q (x –) Q J 10 (x –) Q J 9 (x –)	Queen	Either A K Q or Queen high. Holding A K Q the second lead indicates the original suit length: King (13) shows an odd number Ace (14) shows an even number.
A Q J (x –) K Q J (x –) J 10 9 (x –) J 10 8 (x –)	Jack	A Q J or K Q J or Jack high. Holding K Q J, the second lead indicates the original suit length: Queen (12) shows an even number King (13) shows an odd number.

A Q 10 9 (x –)	Ten	Two higher honours or 10 high.
A J 10 (x –)		With two higher cards this
K J 10 (x –)		sequence is an intermediate one.
10 9 (x –)		

A 10 9 (x –)	Nine	Two higher honours or 9 high.
K 10 9 (x –)		The honours will not be in
Q 10 9 (x –)		sequence.
9 8 x		

LEADS LATER IN THE PLAY

A K J (x –)	Ace	As a rule the lead shows A K (J). However, if dummy has the Queen or the Jack, the King should be led from A K. An Ace lead in this case denies the King.
K Q 10 (x –)	King	Unambiguous.
K Q (x –)		

The lead from other sequences follows the rule for opening leads, except that there may be only a partial sequence such as Q J x or J 10 x.

SIGNALLING ON SEQUENCE LEADS

Partner's action after a sequence lead depends on various circumstances. One of them, commonly neglected, is the number of cards showing on the table. We examine now the correct play opposite the various types of lead.

Partial sequence A K x –:

```
                    North
                    (1) x x x
                    (2) x x

        West                        East
        A K x (x)
                    South
```

Lead: the Ace.

The lead from A K x is most likely to be made when there has been a 'gambling 3NT' opening. Consider first Alternative 1, with three cards in dummy. Whether the lead is from A K x or A K x x, it is unlikely to run into a four-card suit. If the leader has A K x, then partner will normally hold either four or five cards. Should the leader hold A K x x, then partner will usually hold at least three cards. In any event, a signal showing the count will solve the leader's immediate problem. If declarer can be counted for a doubleton, then obviously it will be right to continue the suit.

In Alternative 2, with dummy holding only two cards, we are up against an entirely different situation. It is now much more important to know who holds the Queen and the signal should be directed to that end.

In other words, a signal to show the count will provide the most adequate information when dummy holds at least three cards in the suit, whereas a positive or negative signal, showing strength or weakness, will be most helpful when dummy has at most two cards in the suit.

Incomplete sequences A K J – K Q 10:

North
(1) x x x
(2) x x

West   East
A K J x (x)
K Q 10 x (x)

South

Lead: the King.

In Alternative 1, with three cards in dummy, a four-card suit held by partner is as good as the complementing honour, because the leader is now in a position to continue the suit from the top, dropping the Queen (or Jack) in declarer's hand.

Furthermore, if the leader holds a five-card suit with these sequences a three-card suit length opposite is sufficient for the leader, independent of the complementing honour. Thus a signal to show the count will generally supply the required information. A problem arises only when the leader holds a four-card suit and partner a three-card suit. In this case a signal to show the count will not locate the complementing honour.

The solution to this isolated problem is that partner should play the complementing honour on the lead whenever both dummy and partner himself hold exactly three cards in the suit. The presumption is that the suit will break 4 – 3 – 3 – 3. An important negative inference arises when the signal shows three cards and the complementing honour is not played.

It is true that when partner holds the complementing honour second he will also have to play the honour for the purpose of unblocking. Leader cannot therefore immediately be certain whether partner holds two or three cards in the suit. This is an uncertainty that leader has to live with. If he has a four-card suit he has to decide whether to continue the suit or not. However, he will have located the important complementing honour and may play another round because on the second lead partner will show his remaining length. With a doubleton left he will play the higher and in many cases this will be sufficiently informative. Similarly, if partner's play on the second lead is the lowest of the outstanding cards, leader will know that his honour play on the first lead was from a doubleton such as Q 2 or J 2.

When leader holds K Q 10 x and partner A x x we are in principle dealing with the same situation. Partner can now head the lead with the Ace, returning the higher of his remaining cards. Leader, missing the lowest card, will then have a clear indication that partner holds A x x.

In Alternative 2, where dummy holds a doubleton, the signalling technique described above is not satisfactory. If partner in this case holds three to an honour, to play the honour may present the declarer with an extra trick. Now a positive or negative signal should be given. The exact method is described later.

Solid sequences A K Q – K Q J :

                            North
                            (1) x x x
                            (2) x x
West   East
A K Q x (x)
K Q J x (x)
                            South

Lead: the lowest of the three honours.

In Alternative 1, where dummy holds three cards, the leader will be anxious to know whether partner has at least three cards in the suit, so a signal to show the count is recommended.

In Alternative 2, with a doubleton in dummy, the leader's need for information is different. If partner holds three cards in the suit, it is important to know whether he has a complementary honour card. Consequently, a signal of the positive or negative type is called for.

It might be thought that x x x x opposite a solid sequence lead would justify a positive signal. However, that is not a perfect solution, as one or two examples will show.

                            North
                            6 2
West   East
A K Q 8   (1) 10 7 5 3
                                                   (2) J 5 3
                            South
                            (1) J 9 4
                            (2) 10 9 7 4

Lead: the Queen.

If East gives a positive signal in both alternatives, West will be left guessing. In Alternative 1 he does best to continue from the top, but in Alternative 2 he must follow with the 8.

                              North
                              6 2

West   East
K Q J 7   (1) 9 8 5 3
                                                   (2) 10 5 3

                              South
                              (1) A 10 4
                              (2) A 9 8 4

Lead: the Jack.

If East gives a positive signal in both alternatives, West faces the same dilemma as in the previous example.

Thus it is not right for partner to give a positive signal with x x x x. In Alternative 1 he must play the 8 followed by the 3, giving the count on the second round. In Alternative 2 he gives a positive signal with the 3 on the first round.

When the leader shows a solid sequence, either A K Q x or K Q J x, a touching sequence, either J 10 x or 10 9 x, can be shown by playing the top card on the sequence lead. Care should be taken, however, not to use this technique if there is any risk that the leader may interpret the Jack or 10 as an unblocking play. Our recommendation is that a sequence play should always be preferred when dummy holds a singleton in the suit, except when partner holds the lowest card or a card that the leader is certain to read as a positive signal.

                              North
                              2

West   East
(1) K Q J 8 5   (1) 10 9 7
(2) K Q J 8 5 4   (2) 10 9 3

                              South
                              (1) A 6 4 3
                              (2) A 7 6

Lead: the Jack.

In Alternative 1 East plays the 10, thereby showing a touching sequence. With West holding a five-card suit, East's play of the 10 is unlikely to be misread by the leader as an unblocking play, as this would place declarer with a five-card suit.

In Alternative 2 East plays the 3, guaranteeing a complementing honour and at least three cards in the suit. In this case the 10 would be ambiguous; it might be from 10 x.

Active cards on sequence leads

In accordance with the rules for use of negative signals, the signalling card should be the third lowest, but the next lowest if the third lowest is an active card.

When the lead is from A K Q x or A K J x partner's 10 or 9 may be active cards when dummy has the 9 or 8.

```
                         North
                         (1) 9 x
                         (2) 8 x
      West                                East
      A K Q 7                             (1) 10 x x
                                          (2) 9 x x
                         South
                         (1) J 8 x x
                         (2) J 10 x x
```

West leads the Queen.

If East plays the 10 or the 9, South will win an extra trick, even though West may turn to another suit. In each case East should play the middle card.

```
                         North
                         (1) 9 x
                         (2) 8 x
      West                                East
      A K J 7                             (1) 10 x x
                                          (2) 9 x x
                         South
                         (1) Q 8 x x
                         (2) Q 10 x x
```

West leads the King.

If East plays the 10 or 9 South will win a trick, even should West turn to another suit. On the other hand, should East retain the 10 or the 9 he may be able later to pin the second card in dummy.

Partner's 9 or 8 may be considered as active cards opposite K Q J x and K Q 10 x when dummy has a doubleton 8 or 7.

	North	
	(1) 8 x	
	(2) 7 x	
West		East
K Q J 6		(1) 9 x x
		(2) 8 x x
	South	
	(1) A 10 7 x	
	(2) A 10 9 x	

West leads the Jack.
East cannot afford the top card in either case.

	North	
	(1) 8 x	
	(2) 7 x	
West		East
K Q 10 6		(1) 9 x x
		(2) 8 x x
	South	
	(1) A J 7 x	
	(2) A J 9 x	

West leads the King.

Again East cannot spare the 9 or 8.

These intermediate cards are normally not 'active' on the second round.

North
(1) 9 x
(2) 8 x

West   East
(1) A K Q 8   (1) 10 x x
(2) K Q J 7   (2) 9 x x

South
(1) J 7 x x
(2) A 10 x x

On the first lead East plays his middle card, because his highest card may prove to be active. However, should West continue the sequence lead, the third-lowest card will no longer be active and should be played as a counting signal indicating two remaining cards. In the examples it will also serve as an unblocking card.

Summary of rules for signalling on sequence leads

On high-sequence leads against a no-trump contract, partner should:

Unblock with an honour second, unless this is bound to result in the loss of a trick.

Give the count if dummy holds at least three cards in the suit.

Play any complementing card, followed by the next-lowest card, if the lead shows an incomplete sequence, and dummy as well as partner holds exactly three cards in the suit.

When dummy is short in the suit, give a positive signal when a complementing honour is held; otherwise, give a negative signal and show the count on the next round.

EXAMPLES OF SEQUENCE LEADS AND APPROPRIATE SIGNALLING

When the lead is the Ace from A K x or A K x x:
Partner shows the count if dummy holds at least three cards in the suit.

North
10 9 8

West   East
A K 7   5 4 3 2

South
Q J 6

West leads the Ace.

East plays high-low and West continues, thus providing East with a long-card trick.

North
8 5 2

West   East
A K 9 7   (1) J 6 4 3
                                  (2) 6 4 3

South
(1) Q 10
(2) Q J 10

West leads the Ace.

In Alternative 1 East plays the 4, showing four cards. (He cannot play the 6 for reasons to which we shall return later). When South drops the 10 West will read the position.

In Alternative 2 East plays the 3, indicating a three-card suit. The correct continuation would now be the 7, ensuring communication between the defenders.

North
9 6 3

West   East
A K 10   (1) Q 8 4 2
                                  (2) J 8 4 2

South
(1) J 7 5
(2) Q 7 5

West leads the Ace, but as he holds the 10 the correct handling of this situation becomes more difficult. In

Alternative 1 a continuation will be right, but not in Alternative 2.

For this reason we vary the counting signal by playing the third-lowest when holding Q x x x and the next-lowest when not holding the Queen. East will thus play the 8 in Alternative 1, and West, reading this as Queen to four, will continue the suit. In Alternative 2 East will play the 4, marking South with the Queen.

Spot cards will not always be as easy to read as in the above example, but the differential use of spot cards to show the Queen fourth or otherwise will generally prove a great advantage.

Positive or negative signal

When dummy holds at most two cards in the suit, partner should give a positive or negative signal.

Because the lead of the Ace could equally well indicate a three-card or a four-card suit, partner has to decide when to use a positive and when to use a negative signal. Holding the Queen he naturally has an opportunity to make a positive signal, but he should also consider how the suit is likely to break.

```
                      North
                      7 4
      West                          East
      Ace led                       (1) Q 8 5 3
                                    (2) J 8 6 5 3
                      South
```

In Alternative 1 a positive signal of the 3 would ensure four tricks opposite A K x x, but not opposite A K x. East therefore has to decide what are the chances of the suit break.

In Alternative 2 a positive signal will provide five tricks if West holds a four-card suit; if he has only a three-card suit, he will nevertheless be able to establish two long tricks. This approach is not useful, however, if East has no entry, and in this event a continuation might give declarer a trick he could not otherwise win.

The best solution is a *modified signal*, occupying an intermediate position between positive and negative, and indicated by playing the *second-lowest* card in the suit. In this way, provided he reads the signal as a modified one, the leader will be able to draw the right conclusion. Modified signalling will not always provide a perfect solution to the problem but is valuable as a basis on which to work.

We turn now to incomplete sequences.

A K J x –
K Q 10 x –   Lead the King

The lead of the King indicates one or other of these incomplete sequences. No other alternatives exist so the lead cannot be misinterpreted.

Quite often partner, by looking at dummy's hand and his own, will be able to see which of the two honour combinations the leader holds. If dummy or partner himself holds the 10, the leader is bound to have A K J. If dummy or partner holds the Jack, the leader will have K Q 10.

Counting signal

According to the rules, partner should give the count when dummy holds at least three cards in the suit. In addition we have the special rule that partner should play any complementing honour card he may hold, usually the Jack, Queen or Ace, when both dummy and partner have exactly three cards in the suit. His next play gives the count (when possible).

These rules provide a key to a frequent and very difficult set of problems, which hitherto have not been properly analysed.

> North
> 6 4 2
>
> West   East
> A K J 8   (1) Q 7 3
>   (2) 9 7 3
>
>   South
>   (1) 10 9 5
>   (2) Q 10 5

West leads the King and in accordance with the rule East plays the Queen in Alternative 1. Having located the Queen, West is now in possession of a very important piece of information, and there is still a chance that partner holds a three-card suit. If West continues the suit East will play the 7, indicating two cards left, as the 3 is still outstanding. When South plays the 5 and the 9 it may be presumed that he does not hold 10 9 5 3.

In Alternative 2 East plays the 3 on the lead, indicating a three-card suit without the complementing honour, the Queen. This informs West not only that South holds the Queen, but that the suit will break evenly.

<pre>
                    North
                    6 4 2

    West   East
    A K J 8 5   (1) 10 7 3
                                    (2) 7 3

                    South
                    (1) Q 9
                    (2) Q 10 9
</pre>

West leads the King.

In Alternative 1 East plays the 3, indicating a three-card suit and at the same time denying the Queen. However, as West holds a five-card suit, he can lay down the Ace, confident that South will drop the Queen.

In Alternative 2 East plays the 7, indicating a doubleton, while South follows suit with the 9 or 10. If East had held three to the Queen he would have played it, and consequently in this case South's Queen must be guarded.

<pre>
                    North
                    6 4 2

    West   East
    K Q 10 7   (1) J 8 3
                                    (2) 9 8 3

                    (1) A 9 5
                    (2) A J 5
</pre>

West leads the King and East plays the Jack. Whether South holds up or wins with the Ace, West will get a count from East on the next lead – in this case the 8, indicating a doubleton with the 3 still outstanding.

In Alternative 2 East plays the 3, indicating three cards without the Jack. Whether South holds up (Bath Coup) or wins with the Ace, West will know the position.

```
                    North
                    6 4 2
West                                East
K Q 10 7 5                          (1) 9 8 3
                                    (2) 9 3
                    South
                    (1) A J
                    (2) A J 8
```

West leads the King.

In Alternative 1 East plays the 3, indicating three cards without an honour. After South has won with the Ace West will know that his suit is bound to run, as East holds three cards.

In Alternative 2 East plays the 9, indicating a doubleton, and West now knows that South holds A J x.

```
                    North
                    6 4 2
West                                East
K Q 10 8                            (1) A 7 3
                                    (2) A 3
                    South
                    (1) J 9 5
                    (2) J 9 7 5
```

West leads the King. When partner holds the Ace, the same signalling should be used as when holding a complementing honour, and consequently East should in each case cover with the Ace. In Alternative 1 he returns the 7, indicating a doubleton, whereupon West recognizes that there is still a lower card outstanding. In Alternative 2 the return of the 3 must be a singleton, and West now knows that South holds J 9 7 5

When dummy holds three cards in the suit, partner, with four cards in the same suit, should always play his third lowest.

North
9 6 3

West   East
(1) A K J 2   8 7 5 4
(2) K Q 10 2

South
(1) Q 10
(2) A J

West leads the King and East plays the 7, his third lowest. This play gives West a sure count of partner's four-card suit. In both cases the 5 would be less clear.

Positive or negative signal

In accordance with the rules, partner should use a positive or negative signal when dummy holds at most two cards in the suit.

A negative signal should as a rule be the *third lowest card* in the suit, but the *next lowest* if the third lowest is an active card.

North
8 4

West   East
A K J 7   (1) 9 6 5 3
                (2) 9 6 3

South
(1) Q 10 2
(2) Q 10 5 2

West leads the King.

In both alternatives East plays the 6, which is the third lowest card in Alternative 1, and the next lowest in Alternative

2, where the 9 is an active card. West reads the signalling cards as negative and turns to another suit. When East obtains the lead he plays the 3 in Alternative 1, indicating three remaining cards, which enables West to cash. In Alternative 2 East returns the 9 on the second round and again West knows the position.

North
84

West
K Q 10 6

East
(1) 9 7 5 3
(2) 9 7 3

South
(1) A J 2
(2) A J 5 2

West leads the King.

In principle the situation is the same as in the example above: East plays the 7 in both alternatives, West reading this as a negative signal. Whether South wins with the Ace or holds up, West will have to wait for a lead from East, the 3 in Alternative 1, the 9 in Alternative 2.

A *positive signal* guarantees an essential complementing honour card. Partner conveys this by playing the *lowest card* in the suit. This technique involves a difference of two cards between negative and positive, and this is important to the leader's reading of the signal.

North
9 7

West
(1) K Q 10 6
(2) K Q 10 6

East
(1) J 4 3
(2) A 4 3

South
(1) A 8 5 2
(2) J 8 5 2

West leads the King.

In both alternatives East plays the 3, his lowest card, which should be interpreted as a positive signal, indicating an adequate honour card. South may conceal the 2, but this in no way misleads West, because East's play of the 3 cannot be a negative 'third lowest'.

When third hand has five cards and there is a doubleton in dummy, a positive signal is correct but may not always be crystal clear.

North
7 4

West	East
(1) A K J 6	(1) 10 8 5 3 2
(2) K Q 10 6	(2) 9 8 5 3 2

South
(1) Q 9
(2) A J

West leads the King, East plays the positive 2 and West has to decide whether East holds three to an honour or five small. There will usually be sufficient indication from the bidding.

We turn next to the lead of the Queen, which signifies A K Q or Queen high:

> A K Q x
> Q J 10 x   Lead the Queen

Because of the big difference between A K Q and Queen high, we assume in the following examples that the lead has been read correctly.

Counting signal
   According to the rules, partner should show the count when dummy has at least three cards in the suit.

North
8 6 4 3

West	East
A K Q 7	9 5 2

South
J 10

West leads the Queen and on East's play of the 2 he cashes the Ace. On the third round he plays low to East's 9.

> North
> 7 5 2

West
A K Q 9

East
(1) 10 3
(2) 10 6 3

> South
> (1) J 8 6 4
> (2) J 8 4

West leads the Queen.

In Alternative 1 East plays the 10, indicating a doubleton and also unblocking. In Alternative 2 East plays the 3, indicating a three-card suit, and West now knows that he has four top tricks.

> North
> 6 5 3

West
Q J 9 7

East
10 4 2

> South
> A K 8

West leads the Queen.

East, holding the 10, has a complementing honour to West's sequence, and as dummy has three cards in the suit he should play the 10.

Positive or negative signal

When dummy holds at most two cards in the suit, partner gives a positive or negative signal. He shows the count on the second round (when possible).

North
10 2

West   East
(1) A K Q 4   (1) 9 6 3
(2) A K Q 8   (2) 9 6 3
(3) A K Q 7   (3) 9 8 3

South
(1) J 8 7 5
(2) J 7 5 4
(3) J 6 5 4

West leads the Queen.

On a lead from A K Q x, the 9 may be an active card when dummy holds the 8, but not when dummy holds the 10. Here East plays the 9 in each case.

In Alternative 1 West will know that South holds J x x x because the 9 must be both the third lowest and also the highest card in East's hand. For this reason the suit cannot possibly yield more than three tricks, and West will have to work out a defensive strategy based on this knowledge. It is true that the 9 may assist South to develop a trick, but he might do this anyway.

In Alternative 2 West knows that South holds J x x x, but in this case he cashes the second honour, retaining a major tenace.

In Alternative 3 West knows that the suit will not run as South holds four to the Jack. The problem now, however, is to decide who has the 8. West will have to make up his mind about this, and if he reckons that the defence has the best chance in the suit he will cash the second honour before turning to another suit. On the second round East plays the 8, which confirms the count and unblocks.

North
5 3

West
À K Q 6

East
(1) 9 7 4 2
(2) J 7 4

South
(1) J 10 8
(2) 10 9 8 2

West leads the Queen.

In Alternative 1 East plays the 7, West continues the suit, and East plays the 2, indicating three remaining cards.

In Alternative 2 East plays the 4, which West interprets as a positive signal. He continues with the 6 and makes four tricks.

North
7 4

West
(1) Q J 9 6
(2) Q J 10 8

East
(1) 10 5 3
(2) 6 5 3 2

South
(1) A K 8 2
(2) A K 9

West leads the Queen.

In Alternative 1 East, who holds the complementing 10, gives a positive signal by playing the 3. West can underlead at his first opportunity.

In Alternative 2 East plays the 5, which West reads as a negative signal. Next time either West or East is in the lead East will play the 2 to confirm that he has three remaining cards in the suit.

If dummy holds a singleton, situations may arise which can be solved only by accurate defensive play in accordance with the detailed rules. Here is an example:

North
8

West   East
(1) A K Q 5   10 9 4 3
(2) A K Q 5 2

South
(1) J 7 6 2
(2) J 7 6

West leads the Queen.

East can see that West has led from A K Q (not from Q J 10 or Q J 9). As the 10 9 may be needed, East plays the 4.

In Alternative 1 West continues with the Ace, an even card, indicating a four-card suit (originally) and East plays the 3. This signal enables West to infer that South holds four to the Jack and for the following reason: East cannot hold the Jack and must consider his third lowest card to be active – undoubtedly the 9 accompanied by the 10.

In Alternative 2 West continues with the King, showing a five-card suit (originally). East now plays the 10 to avoid blocking the suit. As East's play is not consistent with an original holding of 10 9 x or 10 x x, West will easily read his partner for 10 9 x x.

The lead of the Jack, it will be remembered, signifies A Q J, K Q J, or Jack high:

A Q J x
K Q J x   Lead the Jack
J 10 9 x

The difference in honour points between A Q J and K Q J on the one hand and J 10 9 on the other is such that there should be no difficulty in reading this lead correctly so far as the two main alternatives are concerned. Nor does it matter whether partner interprets the lead to mean A Q J or K Q J, since the need for information will in principle be the same, the 10 being an important card. In the following examples we presuppose a correct reading of the lead.

Counting signal

According to the rules partner should use the counting signal if dummy holds at least three cards in the suit.

```
                      North
                      8 5 4 2
West                                  East
K Q J 7                               9 6 3
                      South
                      A 10
```

West leads the Jack and East plays the 3, indicating three cards in the suit. If South wins the first trick West will know the position later when the 10 falls under the Queen.

```
                      North
                      7 5 2
West                                  East
K Q J 8                               (1) 9 4
                                      (2) 9 6 4
                      South
                      (1) A 10 6 3
                      (2) A 10 3
```

West leads the Jack.

In Alternative 1 East plays the 9, indicating a doubleton and marking South with A 10 x x. In Alternative 2 East plays the 4, indicating an odd number.

```
                      North
West                  8 5 2            East
J 10 9 7 3                             K 6 4
                      South
                      A Q
```

West leads the Jack and East plays the 4, indicating three cards in the suit. When South wins with the Queen, West knows all.

Positive or negative signal

When dummy holds at most two cards in the suit, partner should use a positive or negative signal depending on whether or not he holds a critical honour.

                    North
                    9 3

West   East
K Q J 6   (1) 8 7 4
                                            (2) 8 7 5 4
                                            (3) 10 5 4

                    South
                    (1) A 10 5 2
                    (2) A 10 2
                    (3) A 8 7 2

West leads the Jack.

In Alternative 1 East plays the 8, his third-lowest, denying the 10 or Ace.

In Alternative 2 East plays the 7 and South the 2. West should now realise that two cards lower than the 7 are still outstanding and that East probably holds at least one of them. It is, however, unlikely that South holds A 10 8 2 as he did not capture the lead, and for this reason it is most likely that East holds 8 7 x x. West will therefore continue the suit, East confirming his three remaining cards by playing the 4.

In Alternative 3 East plays the 4, a positive signal. West will follow with the 6, in the certainty that he will find a touching honour in East's hand.

                    North
                    (1) 10 6
                    (2) 10

West   East
K Q J 5   9 4 3 2

                    South
                    (1) A 8 7
                    (2) A 8 7 6

West leads the Jack.

With 10 x in dummy East's 9 merits a positive signal of the 2. It would be the same with 9 x x.

North
7

West   East
(1) K Q J 5   9 8 4 3
(2) K Q J 5 2

South
(1) A 10 6 2
(2) A 10 6

West leads the Jack.

As the 9 8 might be valuable East plays the 4, and South holds up the Ace.

In Alternative 1 West continues with the Queen, showing a four-card suit (originally), while East plays the 3, thus confirming weakness and a four-card suit. Whether South holds up or not, West can read his partner's holding.

In Alternative 2 West continues with the King, showing a five-card suit (originally). East now plays the 9 to avoid blocking, and South wins with the Ace. If he examines the alternatives West will easily read the position.

The 10 (like the Jack and Queen) signifies two higher honours or no higher card:

A Q 10 9
A J 10 x
K J 10 x   Lead the 10
10 9 x

There will generally be clues to the exact holding.

Partner's play on the sequence lead

The general rule for partner's play on a sequence lead applies: show the count when dummy has at least three cards in the suit, and give a positive or negative signal when dummy holds at most two cards in the suit.

There are numerous possibilities now, giving rise to different inferences. For example:

```
                  North
                  7 5 3
West                              East
A Q 10 9                          8 6 2
                  South
                  K J 4
```

West leads the 10.

East plays the 2 and South takes the trick with the Jack. In a case of this kind East will need only to decide between A Q 10 9 and 10 9 x.

West, for his part, interprets East's play of the 2 as meaning that he holds three cards, in which case South must hold the King guarded.

```
                  North
                  K 4
West                              East
A J 10 7                          9 6 5 2
                  South
                  Q 8 3
```

West leads the 10.

East, holding the 9 and seeing the King in dummy, realises that the lead must be from A J 10 x. East plays the 6, his third-lowest, and on the next round the 2.

```
                  North
                  Q 3
West                              East
10 9 8 6                          A 5 2
                  South
                  K J 7 4
```

West leads the 10.

In this case the lead must be either from K J 10 x or from 10 9 x. East will usually be able to determine which is more likely. In any case he will play the 2 if dummy plays low.

North
J 3

West   East
10 9 8 6   A 5 2

South
K Q 7 4

West leads the 10.

Since dummy holds the Jack and East the Ace, the lead is bound to be from 10 9 x. If dummy plays low, East will play the 2, as a positive signal, and this will enable West to establish two tricks at a later stage. Should dummy play the Jack, East will win and return the 5.

The 9 denotes 9 high or an intermediate sequence:

A 10 9 x
K 10 9 x
Q 10 9 x   Lead the 9
9 8 x

Partner's play on the sequence lead

The general rule for partner's play is the same: show the count when dummy holds at least three cards in the suit and give a positive or negative signal when dummy has at most two cards in the suit.

North
J 8 5

West   East
K 10 9 7   Q 4 2

South
A 6 3

West leads the 9.

In this case the lead is bound to be either from A 10 9 x or K 10 9 x, because dummy holds the 8, which excludes the possibility of the sequence 9 8 x. If dummy plays low then East too plays low, and South wins with the Ace. When East gains the lead he can play the Queen, confident of finding West with the King.

                         North
                         Q J 10 5
     West   East
     9 8 2   A K 7 4
                         South
                         6 3

West leads the 9.

This situation illustrates the value of being able to
distinguish 9 8 x from, say, 9 6 2. When dummy covers the 9
with the 10 East will take the trick with the King and return
the 4.

     K Q x   Lead the Queen (rarely)
     Q J x   Lead the Jack (rarely)

Sometimes there is no better choice than a lead from a
partial sequence such as K Q x or Q J x.

It is very important that a lead from K Q x should not be
confused with a lead from one of the incomplete sequences,
A K J x or K Q 10 x.

Partner's play on the sequence lead
   *When reading the lead of the Queen, partner should realise that this
might be an irregular lead from K Q x. Even so, he must play according
to the rules, using a counting signal when dummy has at least three cards
in the suit and a positive or negative signal when dummy has at most two
cards in the suit.*

                         North
                         A J 9
     West   East
     K Q 6   8 7 5 4 2
                         South
                         10 3

When West, having no better alternative, chooses a lead of
the Queen, East will know that the sequence lead is from K Q x.
As usual, he should play the 2 to indicate a five-card suit.

Through the use of this counting signal West will be in a position to judge the chances of establishing long cards in East's hand.

                    North
                    10 3
West   East
K Q 7   J 8 5 4 2
                    South
                    A 9 6

In this case East, holding the Jack, will interpret a lead of the Queen as indicating K Q x in partner's hand, as it is highly unlikely that West holds the genuine sequence A K Q x. Since dummy holds only two cards in the suit East will make a positive signal by playing the 2, showing a touching honour to the leader's sequence. On winning the first trick, West can continue the suit.

SEQUENCE LEADS IN SUIT CONTRACTS

Before elaborating our system of sequence leads and signalling on sequence leads, we ought to take a closer look at the most important – and probably the most frequent – of all sequence leads against trump contracts, viz. the lead from a suit headed by A K.

There are two schools of thought on the question of signalling on leads from a suit headed by A K. Standard practice is to give an encouraging signal with a doubleton or the Queen. More modern use of counting signals indicates suit length, whether partner holds a doubleton or the Queen. Neither of these methods can be guaranteed to work satisfactorily.

North
J 5 3

West   East
A K 10 9 4   (1) 8 2
                                  (2) Q 8 2

South
(1) Q 7 6
(2) 7 6

West leads an honour card, conventionally indicating that he holds A K – (this sign indicating A K and others).

Using standard signalling practice, partner would make an encouraging signal in both alternatives, making no distinction between distributional strength and honour strength. This means that the leader will continue the suit. In Alternative 1 the result of this strategy would be favourable, but in Alternative 2 the play might cost a tempo.

In this instance the other system, showing the count, works better. East shows a doubleton with the 8, three cards with the 2.

Note, however, that this method is inefficient in examples such as the following:

North
7 5 3

West   East
A K J 9   (1) 8 6 2
                                  (2) Q 8 6 2

South
(1) Q 10 4
(2) 10 4

West leads an honour card, conventionally indicating A K x.

By playing the 2 East indicates in Alternative 1 that he holds three cards, but this does not give the leader adequate information. He knows that East cannot hold a potential ruffing trick but he has no information about the Queen. In

Alternative 2, however, the counting signal indicates a four-card suit, which means that only two tricks can be won.

Using standard procedure, East gives a discouraging signal in Alternative 1, which is sufficient to indicate that he holds neither a doubleton nor the Queen, and as a result the situation can be dealt with appropriately. In Alternative 2, however, he will probably give an encouraging signal, on the assumption that West holds A K third. The result of this may be the loss of an important tempo.

To cope with this problem we propose a brand-new sequence technique:

> When leading from A K –, the *leader* must inform his partner whether he holds an even or an odd number in the suit. This enables partner to determine immediately how many tricks the defenders are in a position to take.
>
> Partner must in return indicate the number of tricks obtainable – one, two or three.

This style is for opening leads only. Later in the play – after trumps have been drawn, at any rate – the partner will show the Queen by a positive signal. There follows:

> A new table for opening leads.
>
> A new table for later leads.

TABLE FOR OPENING LEADS AGAINST SUIT CONTRACTS

Holding in suit	*Lead*	*Reading*
A K (x –)	Ace	Leader has an even number in suit (A = 14)
	King	Leader has an odd number in suit (K = 13)
		Exception: against slam contracts the lead from A K should always be the King, partner using the counting signal.

K Q J (x –) K Q (alone)	King	Ambiguous: partner should read this as a counting lead from A K, unless dummy or partner has the Ace. The second lead or play indicates the original suit length. Queen (12) shows an even number. Jack (11) shows an odd number.
A K Q (x –) K Q x (x –)	Queen	Ambiguous: partner should read the lead as K Q x (see below for rules for partner's play on the lead). Holding A K Q, the second lead indicates the original suit length. King (13) shows an odd number. Ace (14) shown an even number.
Q J x (x –)	Jack	Unambiguous.
J 10 x (x –) A J 10 (x –) K J 10 (x –)	10	Always accompanied by the Jack.
10 9 x (x –) A 10 9 (x –) K 10 9 (x –) Q 10 9 (x –)	9	Always accompanied by the 10.
9 8 x (x –) K 9 8 (x –) Q 9 8 (x –) J 9 8 (x –)	8	Always accompanied by the 9.

Comments

The new table for sequence leads against trump contracts is devised with a view to providing a maximum amount of important information in as unambiguous a way as possible.

The counting lead from A K introduces a brand new sequence technique. The advantage of this technique will be explained below, in connection with partner's play on sequence leads.

The complete sequence K Q J offers approximately the same strength as A K, producing two certain tricks, provided the break is favourable. It is for this reason that we use the same lead from K Q J as from A K.

The partial sequence K Q x must be distinguished from the far stronger sequence K Q J. Now the Queen is led. This sequence will need support from partner, the Jack being the key card in this connection.

The solid sequence A K Q needs no support from partner. In this case the usual lead should be the Queen, which will inform partner that the leader holds this strong sequence. With a long suit, however, it will sometimes be tactically better to lead the King or Ace to obtain the count.

SIGNALLING ON A LEAD FROM A K

The counting lead from A K informs partner whether the leader holds an even or an odd number in the suit. It is now partner's duty to indicate how many tricks the defenders are capable of making in the suit – either one trick, or two tricks, or three tricks.

If dummy holds at least three cards, including the Queen in the suit, the leader is only interested in knowing how the suit will break. A *counting signal* is therefore demanded.

If dummy holds at least three cards without the Queen in the suit three tricks may be won straightaway in two ways: either with two honour cards and a ruff, if partner holds at most a doubleton in the suit, or with three honour cards, if partner has the Queen. In addition to this, however, there is a third possibility of making three tricks, arising when partner holds J 10 x. To order to inform the leader whether these possibilities of making three tricks do in fact exist, we introduce a brand new signal: *the trick counting signal*.

If dummy holds two cards in the suit, one of which may or may not be the Queen, it will not be possible to make three tricks, owing to dummy's ruffing position, unless partner is able to overruff. However, the new trick counting signal should be used in this situation too, as it will inform the leader how many losers the declarer holds in his closed hand. This gives the leader a better chance to plan the defence. For example, it may be advisable to switch to the trump suit.

Finally, if dummy has a singleton in the suit, partner's signalling should be either a trick counting signal or a suit preference signal, according to rules described below.

When partner leads Ace or King, indicating an even or odd number, third hand should:

1. Use a *counting signal* when dummy has at least three cards, including the Queen.
2. Use a *trick counting signal* on all other occasions, by signalling as follows:
   (a) Playing the lowest card (low-high) indicates that the defenders *can make either one or three tricks (depending on whether declarer is likely to hold a singleton or three cards)*. The three tricks may be the top honours, or through a doubleton and a ruff, or when third hand holds J 10 x and declarer Q x x.
   (b) Playing in principle the third lowest card when two tricks may be expected, but not more. Declarer may be marked with a doubleton or with a guarded Queen.

This example shows why a special system is used when dummy holds Q x x:

	North Q 8 2	
West A K 10 6		East (1) 7 5 3 (2) 9 7 5 3
	South (1) J 9 4 (2) J 4	

West leads the Ace, indicating a four-card suit.

Using a counting signal when dummy has Q x x, East plays the 3 in Alternative 1 and the 7 in Alternative 2, indicating a three-card suit or a four-card suit respectively. West now knows that the declarer will have no discard on dummy's Queen in Alternative 1, whereas in Alternative 2 there will be a discard.

Using trick counting signals, East would play the 7 – his third lowest – in both alternatives. This would not give West the same accurate information on whether South holds two or three cards.

Examples of the counting signal
According to the rule partner should use a counting signal when dummy holds the Queen and at least two other cards.

When partner has a four-card suit he should play the third lowest, making it quite clear to the leader that he has an even number in the suit.

North
Q 10 8 5

West
A K J 2

East
(1) 9 7 6 4
(2) 9 6 4
(3) 9 6

South
(1) 3
(2) 7 3
(3) 7 4 3

West leads the Ace.

Assuming that the leader, on the basis of the bidding, is in a position to read the exact break in each case, his reading will be as follows:

In Alternative 1 East plays the 7, his third lowest, which makes it obvious that East holds an even number, in fact a four-card suit.

In Alternative 2 East plays the 4, indicating a three-card

suit. Whether South plays the 3 or the 7, West will know that East cannot hold a four-card suit.

In Alternative 3 East plays the 9, clearly indicating a doubleton.

Examples of the trick counting signal

We now analyse this brand-new signalling technique in detail, illustrating the various kinds of problem which it solves.

(a) Leader and dummy together hold eight cards in the suit.

```
                    North
                    J 4 2
        West                        East
        A K 10 9 6                  (1) 8 3
                                    (2) 8 7 5 3
                    South
                    (1) Q 7 5
                    (2) Q
```

West leads the King.

East, reading the lead as a five-card suit, plays the 3 (low-high) in both alternatives. In Alternative 1 he calculates that the defenders can make three tricks by way of – Ace, King and a ruff. In Alternative 2 he places declarer with a singleton, as he himself has a four-card suit, and so in this case he is signalling one trick.

Assuming that he can spot a difference of two cards in declarer's hand in the suit, as a result of the bidding, the leader's reading will be:

In Alternative 1 partner's indication of three potential tricks must mean that he holds a doubleton.

In Alternative 2 partner's indication of only one potential trick obviously means that declarer holds a singleton.

```
                        North
West                    10 8 4 2              East
A K J 9                                       7 6 3
                        South
                        Q 5
```

West leads the Ace.

Reading the Ace as an indication that his partner holds four cards in the suit, East plays the 7 (high-low), indicating a potential two tricks, as South is bound to hold only two cards in the suit. West's reading of this card is based on the following reasoning: the 7 is a high-low signal; it excludes the possibility of a doubleton, and also of a four-card suit, as then only one trick would be possible. Clearly South holds two cards in the suit. Initially West has no idea who holds the Queen, but this will soon become apparent.

```
                        North
                        9 4
West                                          East
A K 10 7 6 3                                  8 2
                        South
                        Q J 5
```

West leads the Ace.

Reading the lead as a six-card suit (bid by West), East plays the 2, indicating a potential of three tricks *in relation to declarer's closed hand*. The fact that dummy might ruff high does not affect the signal. West continues the suit, killing the established Queen by means of a potential ruff by East.

(b) Leader and dummy hold less than eight cards in the suit.

This is the commonest and most interesting example of the trick counting signal. It offers the possibility of winning three tricks in any one of three ways.

When partner holds a doubleton, or Q x x, three tricks can be made straightaway by continuing the suit. On the other hand, when partner holds J 10 x, winning three tricks will depénd on whether he can gain the lead to play through the Queen. This is the scheme:

The leader should interpret a low-high signal as a guarantee of three tricks (or one) whenever the Jack or 10 is visible.

                        North
                        9 5 3

West   East
A K 10 7   (1) J 8 4
                                                (2) Q 8 4

                        South
                        (1) Q 6 2
                        (2) J 6 2

West leads the Ace.

In Alternative 1 East plays the Jack. West, holding A K 10 x knows at once that three tricks are theoretically available.

In Alternative 2 East plays the 4. If South plays the 6 West can still count on three plain tricks, because the 4 cannot be partner's third-lowest card.

                        North
                        J 8 2

West   East
A K 3   Q 10 6 5

                        South
                        9 7 4

West leads the King.

Whether West holds a three-card suit or a five-card suit, East must play the 5, his lowest, because the defenders are certain of winning either three tricks or one trick.

The reading of the 5 as a low-high signal cannot be prejudiced by South playing the 7 or 9, because the 5 cannot possibly be partner's third lowest card. Furthermore, since dummy holds the Jack, this excludes the possibility of an active card in East's hand calling for the next lowest card to be played. Consequently the 5 must be East's lowest card. In this case West would continue the suit, and three tricks are a certainty.

North
10 7 3

West   East
A K 9 6   J 4 2

South
Q 8 5

West leads the Ace.

East must play the 4, because with dummy holding the 10 the Jack is an active card. In reading this signal West should be aware of the possibility of partner holding J x x. West has to decide whether East holds J 4 2 or Q 8 4 (or Q 5 4).

The leader's play in such a situation will depend on whether it seems likely that the declarer will eventually have to play the suit himself. If so, it may be safe to wait.

North
7 5 3

West   East
A K 8 6   J 10 2

South
Q 9 4

West leads the Ace.

In this case East plays the 2, his lowest, because, as he holds the sequence J 10 x, there is a chance of making three tricks.

In this and similar situations, the leader's reading of the signal is influenced by the fact that neither dummy nor the leader holds the Jack or the 10. In this case the signal means that the defenders can make three tricks either directly or potentially. The leader must decide whether the situation demands the taking of three tricks immediately. If West does follow with the King East will of course drop the Jack on the second round, denying the Queen.

North
7 5 2

West   East
A K 8 4   (1) J 10 9
                                        (2) Q 10 9

South
(1) Q 6 3
(2) J 6 3

West leads the Ace.

In both cases East will play the 9 and West will know that this means either J 10 9 or Q 10 9. He will have to judge whether it is necessary to seek three tricks immediately.

North
7 5 2

West   East
A K 8 4   9 6 3

South
Q J 10

West leads the Ace.

This situation is the exact opposite of the one shown above. In this situation, if East plays the 9 and declarer an honour card, West is bound to know, thanks to the two-card difference principle, that partner holds the spot cards 9 6 3.

In the examples given above partner's low-high signal was prompted by his holding the Queen or the sequence J 10 x. However, the low-high signal may also indicate a doubleton:

North
10 7 3

West   East
A K J 5   8 2

South
Q 9 6 4

West leads the Ace and East plays the 2.

In reading a low-high signal the leader has to judge whether the signal indicates adequate honour cards or a doubleton, *if he believes this is important to the defence.* Depending on the nature of the hand, it may be wise for West to retain his major tenace.

The aim of signalling on a lead from A K is to indicate whether partner is able to *assist* in winning a third trick in the suit. When he can ruff, but only at the expense of a trump trick, he uses his discretion.

	North	
	(1) Q 5 3	
	(2) J 5 3	
West		East
A K 10 9		8 2
	South	
	(1) J 7 6 4	
	(2) Q 7 6 4	

West leads the Ace.

Let us assume that East holds J 10 9 8 in the trump suit. He should not invite a ruff in either case (unless there are prospects of obtaining two ruffs).

(c) Dummy holds two cards in the suit.

The signal for two or three tricks remains the same. It indicates the number of potential losers in the declarer's hand.

	North	
	10 5	
West		East
A K J 9		8 4 2
	South	
	Q 7 6 3	

West leads the Ace.

When East plays the 8, indicating two tricks in relation to the declarer's closed hand, West will immediately know that the declarer holds the Queen. What is more, in this particular example he will realise that the declarer holds four to the

Queen, since partner's play of the 8 is his third lowest and, in fact, his highest card in the suit. This gives West a precise idea of the cards held by South and will enable him to decide the best defensive play.

North
Q 10

West
A K 8 3

East
(1) J 7 5 2
(2) 9 7 5 2

South
(1) 9 6 4
(2) J 6 4

West leads the Ace.

When dummy holds Q x it may be important for the leader to know whether declarer holds J x x, providing a possible discard on the Jack.

In Alternative 1 East plays the 2, indicating three tricks in relation to declarer's closed hand. This means that East holds the Jack and that South holds at least three spot cards in the suit.

In Alternative 2 East plays the 7, indicating two tricks in relation to declarer's closed hand. This means that the declarer either holds J x x or doubleton.

(d) Dummy holds one card in the suit.

According to our general rule the trick counting signal should also be used when dummy holds one card in the suit, but in this case it may be combined with a suit preference signal.

When dummy holds a singleton it may still be important for leader to know how the suit is breaking, and whether partner or declarer holds the Queen. When dummy holds a singleton the best defence may well be to continue the suit, *provided partner has the Queen*. The trick counting signal in cases of this kind relates only to the Queen.

Higher cards are thus reserved for the suit preference signal, as illustrated in the following example:

                         North
                         7

West   East
A K 10 6 5   (1) Q 9 4 2
                                             (2) J 9 4 2

                         South
                         (1) J 8 3
                         (2) Q 8 3

West leads the King.

The 2 from East indicates that he holds the Queen and is
not a suit preference signal. In Alternative 1 the 4 and the 9
would be suit preference signals. In Alternative 2 the 4 would
ask for the lower suit, the 9 or even the Jack for the higher suit.

In interpreting the signal in a situation of this kind, the
leader should consider the following points:

> A card that is obviously partner's lowest card reveals the
> presence of the Queen and also implies no strong suit
> preference.

> A card assumed not to be partner's lowest card should be
> regarded as a suit preference signal, on the lines laid
> down for this signal.

Communicating

The counting lead from A K and the corresponding trick
counting signal has two aims: *primarily*, to provide information
about the number of winners in the suit; *secondly*, to indicate
the possibility of an underlead.

                         North
                         7 5 4

West   East
A K 10 8   Q J 2

                         South
                         9 6 3

West leads the Ace.

Reading the lead as an indication that West holds a four-card suit, East knows that he and partner hold three winners, and he must now decide whether West or he himself should take the last trick. If he wants West to make the last trick, he should use *the conventional play of the Queen, which will oblige the leader to continue with a small card*. If he prefers to take the last trick himself he can play the 2, indicating three quick tricks.

```
                    North
                    7 6 4
West                                East
A K 10 8 2                          Q J 3
                    South
                    9 5
```

West leads the King.

If East wishes to be in on the second trick, he must play the Queen, calling for West to continue with a small card. If East prefers West to have the lead, once the two winners have been taken, he should play the Jack. West will then know that East cannot have a doubleton J x but must hold either J x x or Q J (x). By playing the Jack, however, East has not called for a low card, so West continues with the Ace. When East plays the 3 on the second round West can read the position and will note that his partner, for some reason, has not played the Queen to ask for an underlead.

```
                    North
                    J 5
West                                East
A K 8 4                             Q 9 6 2
                    South
                    10 7 3
```

West leads the Ace.

East plays the 2, indicating three quick tricks in relation to declarer's closed hand, which must mean that he holds the

Queen. This provides West with the valuable information that
East has an entry and that South has three losers in the suit.

```
                    North
                    10 9 3
West                                    East
A K J 4                                 Q 7 5 2
                    South
                    8 6
```

West leads the Ace.

East, reading the lead to indicate that West holds four cards
in the suit, plays the 5, his next lowest, to indicate two tricks
and the fact that he holds the Queen.

On the basis of the bidding West excludes the possibility
that declarer holds four cards in the suit and as a result he
reads the signal as indicating that East holds either Q x 5 or
Q x 5 2. His best continuation is the Jack, giving East the
option to overtake or not according to his judgement.

```
                    North
                    9 5 2
West                                    East
A K J 6                                 Q 10 3
                    South
                    8 7 4
```

West leads the Ace, and East plays the 3.

Let us suppose that West holds a strong defensive hand,
perhaps A Q J in another suit. By overtaking the Jack with the
Queen and switching to the other suit, East shows that he can
come in again with the 10.

PARTNER'S PLAY ON A LEAD FROM K Q J

The lead of the King may be a counting lead from A K and others or a sequence lead from K Q J. The ambiguity involved does no harm, because the lead of the King should always be interpreted as a counting lead unless the Ace is visible. For this reason we need only concentrate on partner's play where the lead is known to be from K Q J (or theoretically K Q alone).

On a sequence lead showing K Q (J), with dummy or partner holding the Ace, partner should:

> Use a counting signal if dummy holds the Ace.
> Use a counting signal or overtake when he holds the Ace himself.

	North	
	A 6 2	
West		East
K Q J 8		(1) 9 7 4
		(2) 9 7 5 4
	South	
	(1) 10 5 3	
	(2) 10 3	

West leads the King.

In Alternative 1 East plays the 4, which West interprets as a low-high signal, denoting an odd number. If the King wins the first trick West will continue with the Queen, indicating a four-card suit. Dummy wins and East plays the 7. Both defenders know that there is still a winning trick in the suit.

In Alternative 2 East plays the 7, which West interprets as a high-low signal. On the next play in the suit West plays the Queen, whether he is in the lead or not, indicating a four-card suit, and both defenders now know that there is only one trick to be taken.

If partner holds the Ace he must either use a counting signal or overtake, in which case the position is quite clear, apart from the break of the suit. If partner does not head with the Ace, his counting signal must be interpreted by the leader.

                        North
                        9 8 7
West   East
(1) K Q J 4 2   A 6 5
(2) K Q J 4

                        South
                        (1) 10 3
                        (2) 10 3 2

West leads the King.

Let us assume that East wants West to be in on the last trick
the defenders can win in this suit, in which case he must play
his hand as follows. On the lead he plays the 5; in Alternative
1 West continues with the Jack, indicating a five-card suit.
Partner now plays the 6 and West will remain on lead. In
Alternative 2 West continues with the Queen, indicating a
four-card suit. In this case East overtakes and returns the suit.

                        North
                        J 7 4
West   East
K Q   A 10 6 3
                        South
                        9 8 5 2

West leads the King.

The above distribution illustrates a familiar problem. In our
system of sequence leads East realises, since dummy holds the
Jack, that West had led from K Q alone. The standard lead of
the King from K Q would not be clear, as this might be from
K Q x.

When neither dummy nor partner holds the Ace partner must use
the trick counting signal on the assumption that the lead is a
counting lead from A K, with an odd number in the suit.

North
10 6 4

West   East
K Q J 8 3   9 7 5 2

South
A

West leads the King.

East, reading the lead at first as a counting lead from
A K x x x, plays the 2, to indicate one winning trick in the suit,
as he assumes that South is bound to have a singleton
(Queen). When South wins the trick with the Ace, West
knows that the Ace was either single or from A x x, since East,
interpreting the lead as coming from a five-card suit, either
holds four cards (one trick) or a doubleton (three tricks
expected).

North
10 6 4

West   East
K Q J   9 7 5 2

South
A 8 3

West leads the King.

East, reading the lead as A K x, plays the 7, his third-
lowest, to indicate that two tricks are expected. After winning
the first trick West continues with the Jack, indicating a three-
card suit; East plays the 2, indicating three remaining cards,
and South wins. Both defenders now know that there is still
one trick to be taken in the suit.

North
10 6 4

West   East
K Q J 8   9 7 5 2

South
A 3

West leads the King.

In this case partner, assuming at first that the lead shows A K with an odd number, may be in doubt whether the lead is from A K x x x or A K x. When in doubt, the safest course is to assume that the lead is from a three-card suit. The reason for this is that if leader holds a five-card suit declarer will hold the Queen single, and when this is dropped on the first trick the leader will realise that the signal was based on a false assumption. In the present case, East plays the 7 as though two tricks could be expected.

In this case leader cannot read whether partner has a three- or four-card suit; but the second time the suit is played both defenders will know the distribution. West will play the Queen for a four-card suit and East the 2 as a counting signal to indicate three remaining cards.

SIGNALLING ON SEQUENCE LEADS FROM K Q x (A K Q)

According to the rules, the lead of the Queen should be read as K Q x, though leader may occasionally hold the strong, complete sequence A K Q. The feature common to the two sequences, in so far as the need for information is concerned, is that the Jack is a key card when the leader holds K Q x, and an interesting card when he holds A K Q x.

On a lead of the Queen, indicating K Q x (A K Q), partner should:

use a positive or negative signal to show whether he is holding the Ace or the Jack;

use a counting signal if dummy holds at least three cards including the Jack (and also if dummy holds A J alone).

This rule for partner's play on a sequence lead from K Q x or A K Q (x) works well in the great majority of situations. Here are some examples:

North
A 9 2

West
K Q 8 5

East
(1) 10 7 3
(2) J 7 3

South
(1) J 6 4
(2) 10 6 4

West leads the Queen.

In Alternative 1 East plays the 7, high-low for a negative signal, which means that he does not hold the Jack. West will then desist from a further lead in this suit. In Alternative 2 East plays the 3, which marks him with the Jack.

North
9 4 2

West
K Q 10 6

East
(1) 8 5 3
(2) J 5 3

South
(1) A J 7
(2) A 8 7

West leads the Queen.

In Alternative 1 East plays the 8, obviously a high-low signal, denying any honour. Consequently, South is bound to hold A J x. In Alternative 2 East plays the 3, obviously a low-high signal, indicating that he holds either the Ace or the Jack.

North
8 3

West
K Q 9 5 2

East
J 7 6 4

South
A 10

West leads the Queen, East plays the 4, indicating a positive signal, and South heads with the Ace. Should South later on play the suit himself for a throw-in, West will know that partner holds the Jack.

> North
> (1) J 7 4
> (2) A J 7 4

> West
> K Q 9 6

> East
> (1) A 8 5 2
> (2) 10 5 3 2

> South
> (1) 10 3
> (2) 8

West leads the Queen.

When dummy holds at least three cards, including the Jack, partner must give the count. In this case the Jack will be visible and the leader will place his partner with the Ace when the Queen holds the first trick.

In both alternatives East may play the 5, which in Alternative 2 will be his third-lowest, to give West a confident count.

When the leader holds A K Q x he will learn about the Jack, which may prove an interesting card for the purpose of communication.

> North
> 9 4 2

> West
> A K Q 6

> East
> J 5 3

> South
> 10 8 7

West leads the Queen.

When East plays the 3 as a low-high signal West knows he holds the Jack. This card may provide a valuable entry, now or later.

LATER SEQUENCE LEADS AGAINST TRUMP CONTRACTS

Later in the play there is likely to be less interest in ruffing possibilities. Most sequence leads will be from lesser holdings – Q 10 9 rather than A K. Most signals rely on the two-card difference principle.

TABLE FOR SUBSEQUENT LEADS IN SUIT CONTRACTS

Holding in suit	Lead	Reading
A K J – A K x –	Ace	As a rule, the lead shows A K. However, if dummy holds the Queen or the Jack, the King should be led from A K. An Ace lead in this case denies the King.
K Q 10 – K Q –	King	Unambiguous.
A K Q – Q J –	Queen	Ambiguous.
K Q J – J 10 –	Jack	Two or no cards higher than the Jack.
10 9 – A J 10 – K J 10 –	10	Two or no cards higher than the 10.
9 8 – A 10 9 – K 10 9 – Q 10 9 –	9	Two or no cards higher than the 9.

Comments

The table for later sequence leads against suit contracts is similar to the table for later sequence leads against no-trump contracts.

The table distinguishes between the very important sequences A K and K Q. However, if dummy holds the Queen or the Jack, the lead from A K should be the King. Obviously, when dummy holds the Queen, the lead of the King cannot be from K Q, while if dummy holds the Jack the lead of the King cannot be interpreted as requesting support from the Jack. Consequently in these positions the lead of the Ace denies the King.

The most important lead is the one from lower sequences, such as J 10, K J 10 or 10 9, Q 10 9. It will usually be easy enough for partner to distinguish between the two possibilities that exist when the 9 or 10 is led.

              North
              7 6 2

West   East
K J 4   (1) 10 9 8 3
                                (2) Q 10 9 3

              South
              (1) A Q 5
              (2) A 8 5

South is playing a suit contract and East is in the lead.

In Alternative 1 he leads the 10, and in Alternative 2 the 9, in accordance with the rules. In both alternatives South wins with the Ace. Obtaining the lead later on, West now has to decide whether South or East holds the Queen. The new table solves this problem, because in Alternative 1, East's lead of the 10 cannot be from an intermediate sequence, three higher honours having already appeared. On the other hand, East's lead of the 9 in Alternative 2 is clearly from Q 10 9 as South would not have played the Ace from A Q 10.

INDICATING A SEQUENCE WHEN FOLLOWING
SUIT OR WHEN DISCARDING

To indicate a sequence when following suit or when discarding, we have this rule:

> A sequence is indicated by *playing the lowest card* in the sequence when the card *has a possibility of influencing* the trick.
>
> A sequence is indicated by *playing the highest card* in the sequence when the card *will not influence* the trick.
>
> A sequence is indicated by *discarding the highest card* in the sequence.

North
A 8 5

West
6 4 2

East
Q J 10 7

South
K 9 3

South is the declarer and West leads the 2.

If dummy plays low East plays the 10, the lowest card in the sequence, since this card has the possibility of influencing the trick.

If dummy wins with the Ace East plays the Queen, the highest card in the sequence, because the card will not influence the trick.

Conventional play of the Queen

On a sequence lead indicating A K against a suit contract, the Queen is a conventional request for leader to follow with a low card.

North
7 5 4

West
A K 9 8

East
Q J 6 2

South
10 3

South is playing a suit contract.

West leads the Ace.

If East, reading the lead as a four-card suit, wishes to obtain the lead on the next trick, he must play the Queen, demanding a spot card on the next round.

Indicating a sequence and the suit length

When holding a complete sequence, the sequence as well as the suit length may be indicated:

A K Q (x –)   The first play is the Queen. The next play may now indicate the length of the suit (original length):
The King (13) indicates an odd number
The Ace (14) indicates an even number.

K Q J (x –)   The first play is the Jack. The next play may now indicate the suit length (original length):
The Queen (12) indicates an even number
The King (13) indicates an odd number.

When holding A K, the sequence as well as the suit length may be indicated:

A K (x –)   The play of the Ace followed by the King indicates an even number in the suit.
The play of the King followed by the Ace indicates an odd number.

Summary

DISTRIBUTION SIGNALS

The length of a suit is shown by leading (counting lead) or by following suit or discarding (counting signal) in this manner:

2 card suit: high-low
4-card suit: next lowest – lowest } even number
6-card suit: third lowest – lowest

3-card suit: lowest – next lowest
5-card suit: lowest – next lowest } odd number
7-card suit: lowest – third lowest

THE NEW THIRD HAND RULE

On a counting lead from a long suit against a no-trump contract the third hand should play high except in the following case:

If dummy and third hand hold only spot cards in the suit, and the sum of leader's, dummy's and third hand's cards totals eleven, third hand should play his lowest card.

THE NEW TRUMP SIGNAL

The new trump signal indicates the distribution type:
High-low shows that the hand has the distribution pattern: one suit with an even number of cards, three odd.
Low-high shows that the hand has the distribution pattern: one suit with an odd number of cards, three even.

POSITIVE AND NEGATIVE SIGNALS

Positive or negative signals to show strength or weakness should be used:

Generally:

On Ace leads in situations where the defenders are obviously compelled to make their quick tricks immediately.

Particularly:

On Ace leads against slam contracts. The lead denies the King, and asks primarily for the King in partner's hand.

On honour leads, in accordance with the rules for signalling on sequence leads against no-trump contracts and against trump contracts (set out in detail under sequence leads).

A positive signal is given by playing the *lowest card* in the suit.

A negative signal is given by playing the *third lowest* card in the suit but the *next lowest* if the third lowest is an *active card*.

SUIT PREFERENCE SIGNAL

The suit preference signal should be used in situations where the defender in the lead is *obviously* compelled to switch to a suit other than the one played, and needs guidance from his partner.

When partner plays an unusually high card he wants the higher ranking of the possible suits in return.

When partner plays a low card he wants the lower ranking of the possible suits in return.

COMBINED SIGNALLING

The use of a positive or a negative or a suit preference signal should be combined with a delayed distributional signal according to the following rules:

The first signalling card indicates a positive or a negative or a suit preference signal, according to the respective rules.

The second signalling card in the same suit is a delayed distributional signal indicating the remaining length in that suit.

NEW TABLE FOR OPENING SEQUENCE LEADS AGAINST NO-TRUMP CONTRACTS

Holding in suit	Lead	Reading
A K x (x –)	Ace	Partial sequence without other honours in the suit.
A K J (x –) K Q 10 (x –)	King	Incomplete sequence lacking the Queen or the Jack
A K Q (x –) Q J 10 (x –) Q J 9 (x –)	Queen	Two or no higher honours than the Queen. Holding A K Q the second lead indicates the original suit length: King (13) shows an odd number Ace (14) shows an even number.
A Q J (x –) K Q J (x –) J 10 9 (x –) J 10 8 (x –)	Jack	Two or no higher honours than the Jack. Holding K Q J the second lead or play indicates the original suit length: Queen (12) shows an even number King (13) shows an odd number.
A Q 10 (9 –) A J 10 (x –) K J 10 (x –) 10 9 x	10	Two or no higher honours than the 10. With two higher cards the sequence is an intermediate one.
A 10 9 (x –) K 10 9 (x –) Q 10 9 (x –) 9 8 x	9	Two or no higher cards than the 9. With two higher cards the sequence is an intermediate one.

Appropriate signalling:

Unblock with an honour second, unless this is likely to result in the loss of a trick.

Use a counting signal when dummy holds at least three cards in the suit.

Use any complementing card, followed by the next-lowest card, when the lead shows an incomplete sequence and dummy as well as partner holds exactly three cards in the suit.

Use a positive or negative signal to show the existence or non-existence of a card touching the actual sequence, followed by a distributional signal on the next round, when dummy holds at most two cards in the suit.

NEW TABLE FOR OPENING SEQUENCE LEADS AGAINST TRUMP CONTRACTS

Holding in suit	*Lead*	*Reading*
A K (x –)	Ace	When holding an even number (A = 14)
	King	When holding an odd number (K = 13)
		Exception: Against slam contracts the lead from A K (x) should always be the King, partner using counting signal.
K Q J (x –) K Q (alone)	King	Ambiguous: partner should read the lead as a counting lead from A K with an odd number, unless dummy or partner has the Ace. The second lead or play indicates the original suit length: Queen (12) shows an even number. Jack (11) shows an odd number.

A K Q (x –) K Q x (x –)	Queen	Ambiguous: partner should read the lead as K Q x (see below rules for partner's signalling). Holding A K Q the second lead or play indicates the original suit length: King (13) shows an odd number. Ace (14) shows an even number.
Q J x (x –)	Jack	Unambiguous.
J 10 x (x –) A J 10 (x –) K J 10 (x –)	10	Generally unambiguous.
10 9 x (x –) A 10 9 (x –) K 10 9 (x –) Q 10 9 (x –)	9	Generally unambiguous.
9 8 x (x –) K 9 8 (x –) Q 9 8 (x –) J 9 8 (x –)	8	Generally unambiguous.

Note: The lead from A K Q (x) may alternatively be the Ace or the King according to the rules for a counting lead from A K (x –).

Appropriate signalling:

1. On a counting lead from A K (x –) partner should:

Use a *counting signal* if dummy has at least three cards, including the Queen, in the suit.

Use a *trick counting signal* on all other occasions by signalling as follows:

(a) Playing the *lowest card* (low-high) indicates that the defenders can make *either one or three tricks in relation to declarer's closed hand*. The three tricks may arise from a ruff or from the Queen or from J 10 x.

(b) Playing the *third lowest card*, but the next lowest if the third lowest is an *active card*, means that the defenders can make two tricks in the suit, either because declarer has only two cards in the suit, or because partner cannot assist in making a third trick.

2. On a sequence lead showing K Q (J), with dummy or partner holding the Ace, partner should:

Use a counting signal if dummy holds the Ace.

Use a counting signal or overtake when he himself holds the Ace.

3. On a sequence lead showing K Q x or A K Q partner should:

Use a positive or negative signal to show whether or not he holds the Ace or Jack.

Use a counting signal if dummy holds at least three cards, including the Jack, or if dummy holds A J.

TABLE FOR LATER SEQUENCE LEADS AGAINST NO-TRUMP AND TRUMP CONTRACTS

Holding in suit	*Lead*	*Reading*
A K J –	Ace	As a rule, the lead shows A K. However, if dummy holds the Queen or the Jack, the King should be led from A K. An Ace lead in this case denies the King.
K Q 10 – K Q (x –)	King	Unambiguous.

The lead from other sequences is according to the rules for *opening sequence leads against no-trump contracts.*

INDICATING A SEQUENCE WHEN FOLLOWING SUIT OR WHEN DISCARDING

To indicate a sequence when following suit or when discarding, we have this rule:

> A sequence is indicated by *playing the lowest card* in the sequence when the card *has a possibility of influencing* the trick.
>
> A sequence is indicated by *playing the highest card* in the sequence when the card *will not influence* the trick.
>
> A sequence is indicated by *discarding the highest card* in the sequence.

Conventional play of the Queen

On a sequence lead indicating A K against a suit contract, the Queen is a conventional request for leader to follow with a low card.

Indicating a sequence and the suit length

When holding a complete sequence, the sequence as well as the suit length may be indicated.

A K Q (x –)   The Queen indicates the complete sequence. The next play may now indicate the length of the suit (original length):
The King (13) indicates an odd number
The Ace (14) indicates an even number.

K Q J (x –)   The Jack indicates the complete sequence. The next play may now indicate the suit length (original length):
The Queen (12) indicates an even number
The King (13) indicates an odd number.

When holding A K, the sequence as well as the suit length may be indicated:

A K (x –)   The Ace followed by the King indicates an even number in the suit.
The King followed by the Ace indicates an odd number in the suit.

PART TWO

The Early Play

In the first part of the book we have elaborated a design for signalling that should provide the best solution from a theoretical point of view. In this second and subsequent parts of the book we will see how the signalling system works in practical bridge, illustrating this by numerous examples, covering the three main phases into which defence can be divided:

The opening lead, which is the prelude to defence.

The intermediate phase, in which the defenders continue to uncover the secrets of the concealed hand.

The final play. At this stage the defenders should have an accurate picture of the distribution.

OPENING LEADS

A great many contracts stand or fall by the opening lead.

This applies not least to game contracts, which in the modern aggressive style of bidding are often borderline affairs.

Attacking leads aim to maintain the initiative that a lead *per se* will provide. Failure to attack from the very start may well give declarer a decisive advantage. It will enable him to establish his potential tricks before the defenders have rallied their forces for the right attack.

Defensive leads leave the initiative with declarer. The defensive lead aims to give nothing away.

In making a choice between an offensive and a defensive lead, the leader must not consider his own cards only but must try to form a picture of where his partner may have his strength. The weaker the hand held by the leader the more important it is to try and find partner's suit.

Finally it is worth noting that in rubber bridge or team play it may be right to take risks, because overtricks are relatively unimportant; but in pairs play safety is usually the first consideration.

COUNTING LEADS AGAINST NO-TRUMP CONTRACTS

When the bidding suggests that opponents have no fit in a major suit and that they have little to spare in a contract of 3NT, the leader must decide what lead will give declarer the least possible advantage.

```
                    North
                    ♠ J 9 7 6
                    ♡ K 7
                    ◇ A K 7 2
                    ♣ J 8 3
West                                East
♠ 8 5 2                             ♠ A Q 10 4
♡ Q 10 5 3                          ♡ 8 4 2
◇ Q 10 5 3                          ◇ 8 6
♣ 9 7                               ♣ K 10 5 2
                    South
                    ♠ K 3
                    ♡ A J 9 6
                    ◇ J 9 4
                    ♣ A Q 6 4
```

South	North
1NT	2♣
2♡	2NT
3NT	

West must not open up either of the red suits, so the choice is between spades and clubs. A neutral lead from a short suit of three cards is preferable to a doubleton. It is both safer (less likely to 'kill' partner's holding) and better for attack (even

four cards in the opposite hand may be enough). The best lead
here is ♠ 2, indicating an odd number.

As far as East is concerned, the position is now very simple:
he knows that West holds three cards in the suit, so he wins
with the Ace and returns the 4. He now holds a tenace over
dummy's Jack. South, winning with the King, has gained no
advantage and has to play his suits on his own. It is no easy
matter for him to discover just how to handle the various suits
in order to win his contract. In practice he is likely to go down.
Any other lead (especially ♣ 9) is disastrous for the defence.

When no suit is mentioned on the way, the leader should
incline to a five-card suit so long as he has a likely entry card.

North
♠ J 9 5
♡ Q 6 2
◊ 6 3
♣ A Q J 8 7

West
♠ Q 10 7 6 4
♡ J 7 4
◊ K 5 2
♣ 5 3

East
♠ A 8 2
♡ 10 9 5
◊ J 10 9 8
♣ K 6 4

South
♠ K 3
♡ A K 8 3
◊ A Q 7 4
♣ 10 9 2

South	North
1NT	3NT

With Q 10 x x x in spades and a potential entry in the ◊ K,
West has fair attacking chances. He plays the ♠ 4, indicating
an odd number, which East can easily read to be five. Thus
East has no hesitation in clearing the spades and playing a
third round when in with the ♣ K. He is not tempted to try the
◊ J.

Special considerations may arise when opponents are likely to hold at least one five-card suit. We are thinking of such sequences as:

	South	North
(a)	1 ♡	1 ♠
	2NT	3NT
(b)	1 ♠	2 ♣
	2NT	3NT
(c)	1 ♡	2 ◊
	3NT	

Now an attacking lead is indicated except perhaps when leader's hand suggests a bad break in the long suits held by the opponents. If he lacks a fair suit of his own the leader should play for his partner's hand.

```
                      North
                      ♠ K 2
                      ♡ K 10 4
                      ◊ 10 8 6
                      ♣ K Q 10 9 2
      West                          East
      ♠ Q 4 3                       ♠ J 10 8 6 5
      ♡ Q 7 5 2                     ♡ J 8 3
      ◊ K 7 2                       ◊ 5 3
      ♣ 8 6 5                       ♣ A J 4
                      South
                      ♠ A 9 7
                      ♡ A 9 6
                      ◊ A Q J 9 4
                      ♣ 7 3
```

South	North
1 ◊	2 ♣
2NT	3NT

In assessing the chances of the defence, West should bear in mind that he probably has a guard in diamonds. There is a good chance that East will have a trick in clubs. The defenders may gain tempo and establish long cards, either in hearts or in spades. Spades are more promising because East is unlikely to hold five hearts but may well hold five spades. Consequently, West leads the ♠ 3. East wins the first trick and returns the suit.

The declarer's fate now depends on whether he reads West or East for the long spades. If his first play is a diamond finesse he loses the contract. He succeeds if he tries first to attack East by leading the ♣ K. If this holds he must switch immediately to diamonds.

Occasionally partner may have intervened in the bidding: he may have ventured a take-out double, he may have bid a suit, or he may even have doubled the final bid of 3NT. Partner's bids will always provide special grounds for considering what to lead.

North
♠ A Q J
♡ 7 2
♢ Q J 10 8 7
♣ J 4 3

West
♠ 9 8 4 2
♡ 6 3
♢ K 6 2
♣ Q 10 9 5

East
♠ 7 6 5
♡ K Q J 9 5
♢ A 4 3
♣ 6 2

South
♠ K 10 3
♡ A 10 8 4
♢ 9 5
♣ A K 8 7

South	West	North	East
1 ♣	pass	1 ♢	1 ♡
1NT	pass	2NT	pass
3NT			

East's bid of hearts is a strong suggestion that this suit should be led against a no-trump contract. West accordingly leads the ♡ 6.

The contract will now stand or fall by East's move. In deciding what to play he must take one basic item of information into account, viz. that West holds a doubleton in hearts (alternatively 10 8 6). With a doubleton in West's hand, South is bound to hold A 10 8 x. East realises that if he plays the Jack, then South will hold up. Next time hearts are led, South takes the trick, effectively breaking the East-West communication. The only hope for the defence is that South will need to develop diamonds and that West holds the King. East can defeat the contract by inserting the ♡ 9 at trick one.

SEQUENCE LEADS AGAINST NO-TRUMP CONTRACTS

A sequence lead may be either offensive or defensive, depending on the strength of the sequence. A lead from, for example, K Q J x is very definitely offensive, whereas a lead from J 10 9 x would rate as a safe defensive lead.

The lead of the Ace

The lead of the Ace, showing A K x – is unambiguous. Traditionally, an honour lead is not recommended from an unsupported A K. However, recent trends and developments in the technique of bidding make this a good choice on many occasions because players often take a chance when they bid 3NT.

```
                        North
                        ♠ Q 3
                        ♡ Q 8 6 3 2
                        ◇ 8 5
                        ♣ A Q 9 8
West                                        East
♠ 9 8 5 4 2                                 ♠ J 6
♡ K 5                                       ♡ J 9 7 4
◇ A K 10 9                                  ◇ J 7 6 3 2
♣ 10 3                                      ♣ J 4
                        South
                        ♠ A K 10 7
                        ♡ A 10
                        ◇ Q 4
                        ♣ K 7 6 5 2
```

South	North
1 ♣	1 ♡
1 ♠	3 ♣
3 NT	

The ◇ A is led.

According to the rule, partner should use a positive or
negative signal whenever dummy holds at most two cards in
the suit. The requirements for indicating a positive reply have
not been clearly defined, as this will depend on how the lead is
interpreted in each individual situation. In this case, however,
there should be no difficulty: East knows that West has a
minimum of A K x and there is a very good chance that he
holds A K x x. For this reason East gives a positive signal by
playing the 2.

West, for his part, has no difficulty in continuing with the
King upon receiving East's positive signal. It is unlikely that
East holds only Q x x in diamonds and South four diamonds.

The lead of the King

According to the new table the lead of the King can also be interpreted as an unambiguous sequence lead. Admittedly, leader may hold either A K J x or K Q 10 x, but these two sequences have the same structure: they are both incomplete sequences, and this is the important piece of information that the lead of the King will provide.

North
♣ Q 10 9
♡ A 7 6
◊ A J 7 3
♣ 6 5 3

West
♠ K 5 4
♡ J 5
◊ 10 9 6
♣ K Q 10 9 7

East
♠ 6 3 2
♡ 9 8 4 3
◊ K Q 8
♣ 8 4 2

South
♠ A J 8 7
♡ K Q 10 2
◊ 5 4 2
♣ A J

South	North
1 ♠	2 ◊
2 ♡	3 ♠
3NT	

The ♣ K is led.

With dummy holding three cards in the suit, East should use the counting signal and play the 2, indicating a three-card suit. At the same time East denies the Jack, since with three to the Jack, according to the rule, he would have played it. South wins with the Ace, crosses to the ♡ A and takes the spade finesse. West wins with the King and has no problem in choosing which suit to play back.

The lead of the Queen

The lead of the Queen showing either A K Q x or Q J 10 x is ambiguous in theory but seldom in practice.

                    North
                    ♠ A 8 3
                    ♡ 10
                    ◇ A J 10 9 6 2
                    ♣ A Q 5

West   East
♠ J 9 7 6   ♠ Q 5 2
♡ A K Q 3   ♡ 9 8 4 2
◇ K 4 3   ◇ Q 5
♣ 8 4   ♣ 10 9 7 3

                    South
                    ♠ K 10 4
                    ♡ J 7 6 5
                    ◇ 8 7·
                    ♣ K J 6 2

        North   South
        1 ◇   1NT
        3 ◇   3NT·

The ♡ Q is led.

Not having the Jack, a touching honour, East should here give a negative signal, but to retain the valuable sequence 9 8 he should play the 4, his next lowest. West continues with the Ace, to show that he has a four-card suit, and East completes his signalling by playing the 2. This provides his partner with the following important information: in the first place it confirms that he does not hold the Jack; in the second place it shows that, when playing the 2, he held three cards; in the third place it indicates that he has the sequence 9 8. Thanks to this exchange of information both defenders now know that South holds J x x x and will be exposed to a finesse when East obtains the lead.

After the same bidding the hand might have been as follows:

```
                        North
                        ♠ A 8 3
                        ♡ 10
                        ◇ A J 10 9 6 2
                        ♣ A Q 5
        West                            East
        ♠ K 10 6                        ♠ Q 5 2
        ♡ A K Q 5 3                     ♡ 9 8 4 2
        ◇ 4 3                           ◇ Q 5
        ♣ J 4 2                         ♣ 10 9 7 3
                        South
                        ♠ J 9 7 4
                        ♡ J 7 6
                        ◇ K 8 7
                        ♣ K 8 6
```

The ♡ Q is led.

East makes a negative signal by playing the 4, for the same reason as in the previous example. On this occasion, however, West now continues with the King, to show that he has a five-card suit. East, recognising the danger of a block, throws the 9. This cannot mean that he holds J 9 4, as in that case he would have indicated a touching sequence by playing the Jack on the opening lead (J 9 4 is equivalent to J 10 4 when dummy holds a singleton 10). For this reason West continues with the Ace, East completes his unblocking play by dropping the 8, and West defeats the contract with five heart tricks.

An unambiguous lead from a holding of Q J 10 x is possibly of still greater significance, because this lead occurs more frequently. According to the new table a lead of the Queen from Q J 10 x could not be confused with A Q J x.

North
♠ K Q J 9
♡ 10 7 6 3
◇ A J 2
♣ 6 3

West
♠ 8 6 3
♡ A Q 4
◇ 6 3
♣ Q J 10 8 4

East
♠ A 10 5
♡ J 9 5 2
◇ 10 5 4
♣ 7 5 2

South
♠ 7 4 2
♡ K 8
◇ K Q 9 8 7
♣ A K 9

South	North
1 ◇	1 ♠
1NT	2NT
3NT	

The ♣ Q is led.

South takes the first trick with the King and switches to spades. West plays the ♠ 3, dummy contributes an honour and East takes the trick with the Ace. He is now in a position to consider the possibilities open to the defence on the basis of the following information: South's bidding suggests a balanced hand, with a possibility of five diamonds, but without sufficient honour strength for a 15-17 1NT. Apart from ♣ A and ♣ K, it is highly likely that he holds K Q of diamonds, and this places him with 12 honour points. In addition, he is likely to have the ♡ K, but hardly the Ace, as this would have given him a total of 16 honour points. If the contract is to be defeated, there is no point in returning clubs. On the other hand, a switch to hearts offers good prospects, because West most likely holds the Ace and Queen.

On the basis of this analysis, East makes the killing switch to ♡ 5.

The lead of the Jack

The lead of the Jack, which may be from A Q J, K Q J or J 10 9 is ambiguous in theory, but here again the two-card difference (Jack high or *two* higher honours) will generally resolve the problem.

        North
        ♠ 5 3 2
        ♡ K J 7 3
        ◊ 6 5
        ♣ A Q 10 2

West   East
♠ K 6   ♠ Q 10 8 7 4
♡ 9 5 4   ♡ Q 10 8
◊ A Q J 9 4   ◊ 7 3 2
♣ 7 4 3   ♣ 6 5

        South
        ♠ A J 9
        ♡ A 6 2
        ◊ K 10 8
        ♣ K J 9 8

South	North
1NT	2♣
2NT	3NT

The ◊ J is led.

South takes the first trick with ◊ K and lead the ♡ A, followed by a small heart to dummy's Jack. Obtaining the lead with the ♡ Q, East must decide whether to return a diamond or a spade. It is most unlikely that South, holding ◊ A K Q, would seek extra tricks in hearts rather than clubs. So East has no problem – he returns a diamond, expecting four quick tricks from this suit.

It would have been far more difficult to interpret a standard sequence lead of the Queen, which might alternatively have been from Q J 10 x. This means that South, for example, might hold the following hand:

♠ K 9
♥ A 6 2
♦ A K 8 4
♣ K 8 7 3

In this case too, South might reasonably be expected to try to establish the ninth trick in hearts, before East gets a clearer idea of South's hand. In other words, East is faced with a choice: is he to return diamonds or switch to spades?

                                    North
                                    ♠ 7 3
                                    ♥ A Q J 10 8
                                    ♦ 9 4
                                    ♣ K Q 10 8

West   East
♠ J 8 2   ♠ Q 9 5 4
♥ 7 6 5 2   ♥ K 4
♦ K Q J 6   ♦ 8 7 3
♣ 6 3   ♣ A 7 4 2

                                    South
                                    ♠ A K 10 6
                                    ♥ 9 3
                                    ♦ A 10 5 2
                                    ♣ J 9 5

        North   South
        1 ♥   1 ♠
        2 ♣   3NT

The ♦ J is led.

East makes a negative signal, playing the 8, his third lowest. The foundations have now been laid for a precision defence, which will defeat the contract no matter how South plays.

If South takes the trick with the Ace, his best chance is to test the hearts, playing West for the ♣ A should the heart finesse fail. East takes the ♥ K and returns the ♦ 7, which not only unblocks but also indicates that he has two cards left in the suit. In time the defenders take three diamonds, a club and a heart.

It is more likely that South will hold up on ◊ J and ◊ Q. West will then switch to a spade, again establishing five tricks for the defence.

North
♠ 6 4 2
♡ Q 8
◊ K Q
♣ A J 9 7 4 2

West
♠ J 10 9 8 5
♡ A 10 7 4
◊ 8 7
♣ 5 3

East
♠ 7 3
♡ K J 2
◊ J 10 5 4 2
♣ Q 10 8

South
♠ A K Q
♡ 9 6 5 3
◊ A 9 6 3
♣ K 6

South	North
1NT	3NT

The ♠ J is led.

South wins the first trick with the King (playing the Queen would have revealed that the lead was from a holding of J 10 9 x). South now plays the ♣ K followed by a small club to the Jack in dummy, which lets East in with his Queen. East can now interpret West's sequence lead on the basis of the following information: South's standard no-trump opening indicates at least 15-16 honour points. Dummy has 12 points, East himself has 7 points, and consequently West cannot have more than 5-6 points at the most. This means that he could not have led from A Q J x, as this would have counted 7 honour points. In other words, his lead must have been from J 10 9 x. For the defence to succeed, West must have a minimum of

A 10 7 x in hearts. A switch to the ♡ J, the only correct card,
establishes four heart tricks.

The lead of the 10

The lead of the 10 indicates one of the sequences A Q 10 9,
A J 10, K J 10 or 10 9 x. the difference of at least four honour
points between the two main alternatives makes the lead easy
to read.

```
                    North
                    ♠ K 4
                    ♡ 7 5
                    ◊ K J 10 9 2
                    ♣ A J 8 4
  West                              East
  ♠ 7 5 3 2                        ♠ J 10 9 6
  ♡ A J 10 9                       ♡ 6 4 3
  ◊ 7 3                            ◊ A Q 6
  ♣ 6 5 2                          ♣ 10 7 3
                    South
                    ♠ A Q 8
                    ♡ K Q 8 2
                    ◊ 8 5 4
                    ♣ K Q 9
```

South	North
1NT	3NT

The ♡ 10 is led.

South wins with the Queen and finesses ◊ J, losing to the
Queen. There are two possible ways of defeating the contract:
either West has led from A J 10 x in hearts or else he holds
A x x x in spades and the defence will have time to establish
three spade tricks. However if South hold ♡ A K Q J and not
the ♠ A, he must hold enough in clubs to make the contract a
lay-down.

A standard lead of the Jack, possibly from J 10 9 x, would
not be so clear. South might hold:

♠ Q x x
♡ A K Q x
◇ x x x
♣ K Q x

Now a spade switch by East is the winning defence.

COUNTING LEADS AGAINST SUIT CONTRACTS

Counting leads against trump contracts show the length of the suit and may be offensive or defensive.

Short suits
  A singleton lead is always offensive, aiming primarily at scoring ruffs. But even if partner does not hold the Ace in the suit, the lead of a singleton provides a possibility of scoring a ruff, which could easily upset an otherwise safe strategy.

North
♠ 10 6 5 3 2
♡ K Q 2
◇ Q J
♣ A J 4

West
♠ A 9
♡ 3
◇ K 8 7 5 3 2
♣ Q 7 6 3

East
♠ J
♡ J 10 8 7 6 4
◇ 10 6 4
♣ K 9 8

South
♠ K Q 8 7 4
♡ A 9 5
◇ A 9
♣ 10 5 2

South	North
1 ♠	4 ♠

West leads the ♡3. Dummy takes the trick and starts playing trumps. West takes the Ace, and when he now switches to clubs the contract is doomed because declarer cannot make the normal play in this situation without exposing himself to a ruff.

West appears to give nothing away if he begins with Ace and another spade. But now South eliminates hearts, cashes the ◊A, and exits in diamonds, forcing the opponents to open up the clubs.

The lead from a doubleton is not so obviously offensive. Just how to interpret this lead depends to a large extent on the bidding. Clearly a doubleton is a useful attacking lead when partner has bid the suit.

```
                    North
                    ♠ J 9 2
                    ♡ 5 4 2
                    ◊ A K 8 5 3
                    ♣ Q 4
    West                            East
    ♠ K 8 5                         ♠ 6 3
    ♡ 6 3                           ♡ K Q 9 8 7
    ◊ 9 7 4                         ◊ Q J 10
    ♣ J 10 9 6 5                    ♣ A 7 2
                    South
                    ♠ A Q 10 7 4
                    ♡ A J 10
                    ◊ 6 2
                    ♣ K 8 3
```

South	West	North	East
1 ♠	pass	2 ◊	2 ♡
2NT	pass	3 ♠	pass
4 ♠			

West leads the ♡ 6, East plays the Queen and South cannot escape the loss of a heart, a ruff, a trump and a club.

On the other hand, if any other suit is led, South can win. He must first drive out the ♣ A. East switches to a high heart, but South now ducks and the East-West communication is broken.

A lead from a three-card suit in a suit bid by the *opponents* is as a rule defensive. It indicates that the leader is trying to find a neutral lead which gives declarer no particular advantage. There is an inference that the leader is protecting his honour cards in the other suits.

A lead from a three-card suit in a suit bid by partner simply means that the leader is obeying partner's indirect request to lead his suit. At the same time, however, it does mean that the leader has no better lead available, and this in itself may be useful information.

A lead from three cards in an unbid suit is often offensive, but it can equally well be defensive. Partner must always interpret the lead on the basis of the bids.

The most important feature of counting leads is in every case that they provide partner with unambiguous information on the length of the suit. It is particularly important that partner should not confuse this lead with a doubleton lead.

North
♠ J 9 7
♡ A K Q 7 4
◊ J 8 4
♣ 9 7

West
♠ 10 4
♡ J 9 5
◊ 9 7 3
♣ Q 8 6 5 3

East
♠ 5 3 2
♡ 8 6 3
◊ A K 10 6 2
♣ A 4

South
♠ A K Q 8 6
♡ 10 2
◊ Q 5
♣ K J 10 2

South	North
1 ♠	2 ♡
2 ♠	3 ♠
4 ♠	

A lead from ♣ Q x x x x is unlikely to achieve anything. A diamond lead is more promising because West is short in the suit and there is a possibility that East has tricks to make. West, therefore, leads the ◊ 3, naturally without being too optimistic about the opportunities open to the defence.

East realises immediately that he can cash Ace and King because in view of his lead West either has three cards or a singleton. When West follows suit on the second round East tries a low club. Having seen ◊ A K, South is likely to guess wrong.

Long suits

A four-card suit with honour combinations such as Q 10 6 3, K 10 6 3, or even K J 6 3, is a valuable suit offering the possibility of establishing a couple of tricks.

North
♠ Q 4
♡ J 7 5
◇ Q 7 3
♣ A Q J 9 6

West
♠ 8 3
♡ K 10 6 3
◇ J 10 9 5
♣ 7 4 3

East
♠ 10 7 6
♡ Q 9 2
◇ A 6 4 2
♣ K 8 5

South
♠ A K J 9 5 2
♡ A 8 4
◇ K 8
♣ 10 2

South	North
1 ♠	2 ♣
3 ♠	4 ♠

At first sight a sequence lead in diamonds would appear to be the safest solution, but is it aggressive enough? West must assume that declarer possesses sufficient strength in the black suits to win his contract if allowed time. The defenders must aim to develop rapid tricks in one of the red suits before partner's likely trick in spades or clubs has been forced out. In diamonds East must hold two of the three honours if there is to be a chance of wining two tricks. Most players would lead ◇ J, but ♡ 6 in fact demands less from partner. In the present set-up, Q 9 x is enough.

Forcing game

   A five-card suit such as Q 10 x x x, K 10 x x x, K J x x x, is less likely than a four-card suit to establish defensive tricks.

   Nevertheless a five-card suit is an important asset when there is a chance to play a forcing game.

The following general conditions must exist if a forcing game is to be successful:

> One of the defenders must hold at least four trumps (and dummy must be relatively short).

> The defence must hold a long suit and dummy must be unable to control this suit by ruffing.

> The defenders must hold a stopper in at least one of the declarer's suits, so that they can put the forcing game into effect.

If these conditions exist a forcing game will be successful provided defenders exploit the advantage in tempo afforded by the lead.

North
♠ Q 2
♡ 7 3 2
◇ J 9 6 3
♣ A 7 4 2

West
♠ 8 6 4 3
♡ K 6 5
◇ 2
♣ K 10 8 6 3

East
♠ 10 5
♡ J 8 4
◇ A 10 8 7 5
♣ Q J 9

South
♠ A K J 9 7
♡ A Q 10 9
◇ K Q 4
♣ 5

South	North
1 ♠	1NT
3 ♡	3 ♠
4 ♠	

In assessing the opportunities open to the defence, West should take note of his trump length. South's superiority of one trump is countered by the fact that West holds a potential stop card in hearts, South's second suit. It is also probable that South is short of clubs, where he may well hold a singleton. There is a very good chance that a forcing game will prove successful. West therefore leads the ♣ 3 in preference to his singleton diamond.

Once clubs have been led, South has no possibility of winning his contract. His natural play is to win with the ♣ A and finesse the ♡ 9. West comes in with the King and plays another club, which South is compelled to ruff. In this way South's extra length in trumps is counterbalanced by West's stop card in hearts. South runs out of trumps and is bound to go down. Note that a diamond lead, even though it leads to an immediate ruff, does not defeat the contract.

Trump lead

A trump lead, aiming to reduce declarer's chance of scoring ruffs, is particularly effective in the following situations:

When the bidding suggests that dummy is not strong but has short suits.

When the bidding suggests that the trump break is 4-4 and no strong side suit is held.

Against low trump contracts, where the lead of a trump and subsequent continuation of trumps eliminates dummy's trumps and forces declarer to play a no-trump type of game.

In addition, a trump lead may provide immediate information about the distribution of leader's hand.

North
♠ Q 10 7 6
♡ A 4
◇ K Q 8 5
♣ K 10 3

West
♠ A 5 3
♡ K 7 5 2
◇ 9 7 6 3
♣ 8 2

East
♠ 4 2
♡ Q 10 6 3
◇ A J 4
♣ J 9 7 6

South
♠ K J 9 8
♡ J 9 8
◇ 10 2
♣ A Q 5 4

North	South
1 ◇	1 ♠
2 ♠	3 ♣
4 ♠	

The ♠ 3 is led.

In this case the trump lead is highly effective. Declarer can no longer ruff two diamonds in his own hand, because the opponents will play two more rounds of trumps as soon as East gains the lead with the ◇ A. South gives up the idea of ruffing and returns a trump. West wins and leads a third round.

Already East can assess the entire distribution. By his trump signal West has indicated that he has one suit with an odd number of cards, and as he has indicated three trumps he is bound to have an even number in the other three suits, with presumably a doubleton in clubs.

As a result, when South, after playing three rounds of trumps, plays the ◇ 2 to dummy's Queen, East is in no doubt about the correct counter-move; he takes the trick with the Ace and returns the Jack, the only way in which the contract can be defeated.

This does not, however, mean that the fate of the contract is sealed. Declarer, who spots a chance of a squeeze play, heads the return of the ◇ J with the King in dummy and continues with a low heart in this position:

```
                    North
                    ♠ Q
                    ♡ A 4
                    ◇ 8 5
                    ♣ K 10 3
West                                    East
♠ –                                     ♠ –
♡ K 7 5 2                               ♡ Q 10 3
◇ 9 7                                   ◇ 4
♣ 8 2                                   ♣ J 9 7 6
                    South
                    ♠ K
                    ♡ J 9 8
                    ◇ –
                    ♣ A Q 5 4
```

If East plays low, declarer plays the 8, forcing West to part with the King. East is left in control of hearts and clubs and can be squeezed. (South ruffs a diamond and ♠ Q is the squeeze card).

East can foresee this ending and must go up with ♡ Q when the 4 is led from dummy. After this he is not left with the burden of guarding two suits.

SEQUENCE LEADS AGAINST SUIT CONTRACTS

Sequence leads must be as unambiguous as possible, enabling partner to see at a glance what possibilities the suit offers.

The card partner plays on a sequence lead must if possible indicate the distribution of the suit and also whether or not partner holds touching honours to supplement leader's sequence.

Counting lead from A K

This special lead against a trump contract, with the appropriate rules for partner's play, aims to establish how many tricks can be won in the suit.

A counting signal should be used when dummy holds the Queen *guarded*, because in this case leader is interested only in the distribution of the suit.

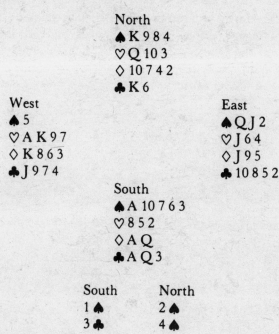

North
♠ K 9 8 4
♡ Q 10 3
◊ 10 7 4 2
♣ K 6

West
♠ 5
♡ A K 9 7
◊ K 8 6 3
♣ J 9 7 4

East
♠ Q J 2
♡ J 6 4
◊ J 9 5
♣ 10 8 5 2

South
♠ A 10 7 6 3
♡ 8 5 2
◊ A Q
♣ A Q 3

South	North
1 ♠	2 ♠
3 ♣	4 ♠

The ♡ A is led.

East indicates a holding of an odd number by playing the 4, his lowest card in the suit. Even if South conceals the 2, West is able to deduce that East has an odd number. Since dummy holds the Queen guarded partner must indicate the holding of a four-card suit by dropping his *third lowest card*. However, East's 4 cannot possibly be his third lowest. No matter what card South plays on the opening trick, West gathers the important information that dummy's Queen does not represent any discard threat, unless East holds five cards in the suit and South a singleton. West can dismiss the possibility, for example, of South holding the following hand:

♠ A 10 7 6 3
♡ 5 2
◇ A J
♣ A Q 10 3

There is therefore no reason to risk a switch to diamonds.

The trick counting signal is used in all cases where dummy does not have the Queen guarded. This technique tells the leader how many tricks the suit will provide *in relation to the concealed cards in declarer's hand.*

North
♠ Q 10 8 4 2
♡ 10 8 5
◇ Q 3
♣ 7 4 2

West
♠ 7 5
♡ A K J 3
◇ 8 7 6
♣ A Q 10 5

East
♠ 6 3
♡ Q 9 6 4 2
◇ 9 5 4
♣ K 8 3

South
♠ A K J 9
♡ 7
◇ A K J 10 2
♣ J 9 6

South	West	North	East
1 ◇	double	pass	1 ♡
1 ♠	2 ♡	2 ♠	pass
4 ♠			

The ♡ A is led.

East interprets the lead as A K to four, and by playing the 2 he warns his partner that they can make only one trick in the suit. This enables West to reason as follows: East's play must mean that South holds a singleton in hearts, because if East had held only four cards in the suit he would have indicated two tricks by playing his third lowest card or possibly the second lowest from Q 9 x x. The best chance is to risk a club from the West side.

Suppose that, consistent with the bidding, South had held the following:

♠ A K 6 5
♡ 9 7
♢ A K J 10 2
♣ K 9

East, with Q 6 4 2 in hearts, would indicate two tricks by dropping the 4. West would read this as a four-card suit, with the Queen as the highest card, and would underlead the ♡ K.

North
♠ J 4
♡ 8 6 2
♢ 10 7 4
♣ A Q J 5 4

West
♠ 6 3 2
♡ A K J 7
♢ A Q J 2
♣ K 10

East
♠ 9 7 5
♡ Q 10 3
♢ 9 6 5
♣ 8 7 6 3

South
♠ A K Q 10 8
♡ 9 5 4
♢ K 8 3
♣ 9 2

South	West	North	East
1 ♠	double	2 ♣	pass
2 ♠			

The ♡ A is led.

East interprets the lead as coming from a four-card suit. He plays the 3, indicating one or three tricks. Knowing that partner holds ♡ Q, West can safely follow with ♡ J. East overtakes and returns a diamond to West's Jack. West, in turn, can read his partner for ♡ 10, so he follows with ♡ 7. This pretty defence, *accomplished without any guessing*, wins the first six tricks.

```
                        North
                        ♠ 8 6 4 2
                        ♡ 10 4
                        ◇ 7 3
                        ♣ A Q J 10 8

        West                              East
        ♠ K 10 9 7                        ♠ J 5 3
        ♡ A 3                             ♡ 6 5 2
        ◇ A K 10 5                        ◇ Q 9 6 2
        ♣ 9 7 6                           ♣ 5 3 2

                        South
                        ♠ A Q
                        ♡ K Q J 9 8 7
                        ◇ J 8 4
                        ♣ K 4
```

South	West	North	East
1 ♡	double	2 ♣	pass
3 ♡	pass	4 ♡	

The ◇ A is led.

East interprets the lead as A K to four. This means that South has three losers and East shows this by playing the ◇ 2. What can West do? There is no point in playing two rounds of trumps; this would allow South to draw trumps and run the clubs. The solution is to lead a low trump at trick two. South can take a discard on the third club, but East can ruff the fourth round and declarer is left with three losers. The trick counting signal, telling West that South has three losing diamonds, is the key to the defence.

When dummy holds Q x in the suit led, the Jack may be a critical card.

North
♠ 10 8 7 5
♡ 9 2
◇ K J 8 6 2
♣ Q 9

West
♠ Q 6 4
♡ K 7 5 4
◇ 10 3
♣ A K 10 5

East
♠ 2
♡ Q 10 8 6 3
◇ Q 9 7 4
♣ 8 6 3

South
♠ A K J 9 3
♡ A J
◇ A 5
♣ J 7 4 2

South	North
1 ♠	2 ♠
4 ♠	

The ♣ A is led.

East indicates two tricks by playing the ♣ 8, his third lowest. West can interpret this card as follows: East cannot hold J 8 x x, because in that event he would indicate three tricks in relation to South's hand by playing his lowest card. Nor can East hold J 8 x x x, because in that case he would have indicated two tricks by playing his third lowest, which could not be the 8. Consequently, East must hold 8 x x and South J x x x. A discard on ♣ J is threatened, so West must immediately switch to hearts.

Alternatively, South might hold:

♠ A K J 9 3
♡ A Q 3
◇ A 5
♣ 7 4 2

Now East, holding J 8 6 3 in clubs, would indicate three tricks in relation to South's hand by playing the 3. The defence then would be to cash two club tricks and exit in clubs.

Lead from K Q J

The complete sequence K Q J is shown by leading the King. By continuing with the Queen the leader shows an even number, while continuing with the Jack shows an odd number (original length of suit).

North
♠ A 10 7
♡ K Q J 5
◇ 10 6 3
♣ K Q 7

West
♠ 5 2
♡ 10 8 6 3
◇ K Q J 9
♣ J 4 2

East
♠ K 6 3
♡ 4 2
◇ A 8 7 2
♣ A 10 5 3

South
♠ Q J 9 8 4
♡ A 9 7
◇ 5 4
♣ 9 8 6

North	South
1 ♡	1 ♠
1NT	2 ♡
3 ♠	

The ◊ K is led.

East sums up the situation as follows: in view of South's bidding, he obviously holds ♡ A x x and probably five spades. This means that there are two possible ways of defeating the contract: the first is if West holds K Q J alone in diamonds, in which case the defenders may win three diamond tricks, one club and one in trumps. The other possibility is for West to hold the ♣ J and South three clubs and two diamonds. To keep both possibilities alive, East overtakes the ◊ K with the Ace and switches to the ♣ 5, on which West plays the Jack and dummy the Queen. Subsequently East obtains the lead with ♠ K and not till then does he play the ◊ 2, indicating that he has three cards left (holding Ace second he would immediately have returned the suit). West, knowing now that there are no more diamond tricks to be won, switches to clubs, enabling East to defeat the contract with two tricks in clubs.

The knowledge that West holds ◊ K Q J enables East to overtake the King and direct the defence.

                    North
                    ♠ A Q J 9 7
                    ♡ 6
                    ◊ 10 8 6 4
                    ♣ 10 7 2

West   East
♠ 10 4   ♠ 8 6 5 3
♡ 10 5 3 2   ♡ 9
◊ K 5 3   ◊ Q J 9 7 2
♣ K Q J 4   ♣ A 9 5

                    South
                    ♠ K 2
                    ♡ A K Q J 8 7 4
                    ◊ A
                    ♣ 8 6 3

            South   North
            2 ♡   2 ♠
            4 ♡

The ♣ K is led.

West holds the first trick and follows with the Queen, to indicate an original even number. This gives East a very precise basis for assessing the chances of defeating the contract. If South holds a club singleton, there is no hope; but if South holds three clubs and so three losers in the suit, the question is where the defence can find the fourth and defeating trick. Most likely this will have to be in trumps, and for this reason East takes the trick with the ♣ A and returns a club. West, who takes the trick with his Jack, is not slow to play the fourth round of clubs, accepting East's invitation to a trump promotion which defeats the contract.

Now imagine that South had held:

♠ K 2
♡ A K Q J 8 7 4
◇ K 3
♣ 8 6

The contract would be defeated just as easily. West would lead the King of clubs, continuing with the Jack, to show an odd number. This excludes the possibility of a trump promotion, since South obviously holds a doubleton in clubs. Consequently the contract will have to be defeated in some other way. East heads the ♣ J with the Ace and switches to the ◇ Q.

Lead from K Q x

The Rusinow principle is used in leading from K Q x (and lower sequences). Partner must use a positive or negative signal to show the Ace or Jack, except that when dummy holds the Jack guarded a counting signal is used.

North
♠ A Q 5 2
♡ 9 6 4
◇ Q J
♣ K J 10 6

West
♠ 7 3
♡ K Q 10 8
◇ 10 5 4 2
♣ A 7 4

East
♠ 8 6
♡ J 7 2
◇ A 9 8 3
♣ 9 8 5 2

South
♠ K J 10 9 4
♡ A 5 3
◇ K 7 6
♣ Q 3

South	North
1 ♠	3 ♠
4 ♠	

The ♡ Q is led and wins the trick. What is bound to worry the leader, after a lead from K Q x has held the trick, is that declarer may hold A J x and be holding up in the hope that the suit will be continued. This problem will be solved by partner indicating positive or negative, depending on whether he has a touching honour or not. In the example shown above, East marks positive by playing the 2, and this enables West to continue the suit.

North
♠ 8 4
♡ 10 7 6 2
◇ A K 7
♣ 8 7 6 5

West
♠ K Q 10 9 3
♡ J
◇ Q J 5 2
♣ K 10 2

East
♠ 7 5 2
♡ A 4 3
◇ 10 8 6 3
♣ J 9 4

South
♠ A J 6
♡ K Q 9 8 5
◇ 9 4
♣ A Q 3

South	West	North	East
1 ♡	1 ♠	2 ♡	pass
4 ♡			

The ♠ Q was led.

As a second spade trick would not be of much advantage, South won with the Ace, crossed to dummy and led a heart to the Queen. When West's Jack fell, South prepared a trap: he played no more trumps but eliminated the diamonds and then played the ♠ J. West won with the King and was now faced with the following situation:

North
♠ –
♡ 10 7 6
◇ –
♣ 8 7 6 5

West
♠ 10 9 3
♡ –
◇ Q
♣ K 10 2

East
♠ 7
♡ A 3
◇ 10
♣ J 9 4

South
♠ 6
♡ K 9 8
◇ –
♣ A Q 3

Reading declarer for 2-6-2-3 distribution, West exited with a club and the contract was made.

Using the modern signalling technique, the defence is a simple matter. When the ♠ Q is led East signals negatively by playing the 7, third lowest. When later South plays ♠ J, East indicates his two remaining cards by playing the 5. This marks South with ♠ 6 and West can safely return spades. When declarer leads a club from dummy, East plays the 9, protecting his partner from a possible end-play.

                           North
                           ♠ J 7 6
                           ♡ J 8 3
                           ◇ A K J 2
                           ♣ A Q 9

West   East
♠ K 3   ♠ 9 8 5
♡ K Q 10 4   ♡ 7 5 2
◇ 8 6   ◇ 10 7 4 3
♣ 10 8 7 3 2   ♣ J 5 4

                           South
                           ♠ A Q 10 4 2
                           ♡ A 9 6
                           ◇ Q 9 5
                           ♣ K 6

        North   South
        1NT   3 ♠
        4 ♠   4NT
        5 ♡   6 ♠

The ♡ Q was led.

The contract should always be defeated but South played in a way that might have proved successful if the defenders had not used the counting signal. He took the opening trick and immediately played three rounds of clubs, discarding the ♡ 9 from his own hand. When West came in with the ♠ K he cashed the ♡ K because the play to the first trick had marked East with an odd number.

Without a counting signal West would have a problem, because South would play the same way with:

                           ♠ A Q 10 5 4 2
                           ♡ A 9
                           ◇ 9 5 4
                           ♣ K 6

Now the defence must play a spade or a diamond, not a heart.

PART THREE

The Middle Game

We proceed now to the intermediate section of the play that begins after the first trick.

SAFETY OR AGGRESSION?

There are two main types of position in defence:

Defensive positions in which defenders choose safe leads to prevent unnecessary loss of tricks.

Offensive positions, in which defenders operate aggressively to exploit their initiative.

Defensive approach

On some hands the best policy is to let declarer make all the running.

```
                    North
                    ♠ K Q 7
                    ♡ A J 9 4
                    ◊ K 6 3
                    ♣ J 7 6

West                                East
♠ 10 9 2                            ♠ J 6 4 3
♡ 5 2                               ♡ Q 10 8 7
◊ Q 10 8 7                          ◊ 5 2
♣ Q 10 5 3                          ♣ K 8 4

                    South
                    ♠ A 8 5
                    ♡ K 6 3
                    ◊ A J 9 4
                    ♣ A 9 2
```

South	North
1NT	3NT

The ♠ 10 is led.

The natural approach – and the one that offers the best prospects – is to try to establish the ninth trick in one of the red suits. The first trick is won on the table. A heart is led to the King and the Jack is finessed on the next round. East wins with the Queen and returns a spade. Nothing is given away. Declarer tries his luck in diamonds, with the same result. The defenders again play spades, giving nothing away. South's best prospects now rest with a favourable break in hearts or diamonds. He plays these suits in turn, without any success, and arrives at this position:

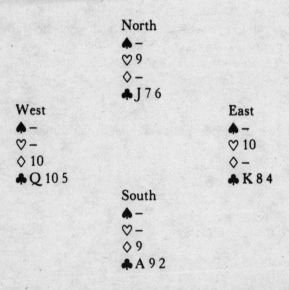

North
♠ –
♡ 9
◇ –
♣ J 7 6

West
♠ –
♡ –
◇ 10
♣ Q 10 5

East
♠ –
♡ 10
◇ –
♣ K 8 4

South
♠ –
♡ –
◇ 9
♣ A 9 2

South exits with a diamond and now West can beat the contract by leading ♣ 10. South is defeated despite a combined holding of 30 points. The contract can be made at double dummy, of course, but the suggested line is entirely reasonable.

Offensive approach

At the opposite end of the scale are those hands where the defenders must attack boldly and quickly.

```
                    North
                    ♠ A 7 4 3
                    ♡ 6 5 2
                    ◇ A 10 2
                    ♣ K 6 2
West                                    East
♠ 10 5 2                                ♠ K 6
♡ Q 8 7 4                               ♡ J 10 9 3
◇ 8 3                                   ◇ K Q 9 4
♣ Q 9 7 4                               ♣ 10 5 3
                    South
                    ♠ Q J 9 8
                    ♡ A K
                    ◇ J 7 6 5
                    ♣ A J 8
```

South	North
1NT	2♣
2♠	4♠

The ◇ 8 is led.

East wins the first trick with the ◇ Q and has to find the best return. The ♡ J looks obvious, but reflect: South is going to obtain a discard on the fourth round of diamonds and, since East can see seven hearts and only six clubs, the valuable discard will probably be in clubs. As can be seen, the killing return is a club, not a heart.

Positional analysis

In the next example the type of defence varies according to the declarer's play at trick one.

North
♠ A Q J 6
♡ 9 4
◇ A 9 7 3
♣ K 9 5

West   East
♠ 8 5 3   ♠ K 10 7 2
♡ 8 6 5 2   ♡ A K 3
◇ Q 8 4   ◇ 10 5 2
♣ Q 8 6   ♣ 10 4 2

South
♠ 9 4
♡ Q J 10 7
◇ K J 6
♣ A J 7 3

North	South
1 ◇	1 ♡
1 ♠	2NT
3NT	

The ♠ 3 is led.

If South chooses to play the Jack, East covers with the King. West's defensive lead has now created an offensive position for East, who returns the ♠ 10, pinning South's 9. Dummy wins and leads the ♡ 9, which holds the trick. East wins the next heart and plays a third round of spades. Not fancying the diamond finesse, South crosses to ◇ K and clears his heart trick. East has the lead in the following position:

                          North
                          ♠ 6
                          ♡ –
                          ◇ A 9
                          ♣ K 9 5

West   East
♠ –   ♠ 7
♡ 8   ♡ –
◇ Q 8   ◇ 10 5
♣ Q 8 6   ♣ 10 4 2

                          South
                          ♠ –
                          ♡ Q
                          ◇ J 6
                          ♣ A J 7

The ♠ 7 now forces South to an uncomfortable discard.

Suppose, instead, that South plays low from dummy on the opening lead. East wins with ♠ 10 and is now obviously in a defensive position. To avoid giving away a trick he plays three rounds of hearts. This produces the following situation:

                          North
                          ♠ A Q J
                          ♡ –
                          ◇ A 9 7
                          ♣ K 9 5

West   East
♠ 8 5   ♠ K 7 2
♡ 8   ♡ –
◇ Q 8 4   ◇ 10 5 2
♣ Q 8 6   ♣ 10 4 2

                          South
                          ♠ 9
                          ♡ Q
                          ◇ K J 6
                          ♣ A J 7 3

South now takes the ♡ Q. East, forced to discard, realises that he must retain his three spades; if not, South may play the Ace and put East in with the King, after which East will be forced to concede a trick in clubs or diamonds. East, however, avoids this trap by discarding the same suit as dummy – either a club or a diamond. By retaining an exit card in spades, East forces the declarer to open up one of the minor suits. This way, South loses two spades, two hearts and either a diamond or a club.

This deal is an instructive example in control:

North
♠ J 7 2
♡ 9 4 2
◇ Q 7 5
♣ A K Q 10

West
♠ A 5
♡ A 7 6 5
◇ J 10 9 8 3
♣ 7 2

East
♠ 9 6 4 3
♡ 10
◇ K 6 2
♣ J 9 8 5 3

South
♠ K Q 10 8
♡ K Q J 8 3
◇ A 4
♣ 6 4

South	North
1 ♡	2 ♣
2 ♠	3 ♡
4 ♡	

The ◊ 10 is led.

Dummy covers with the Queen, East plays the King, and South takes the trick with the Ace. South continues with three rounds of clubs to discard his diamond loser. West ruffs and leads a diamond, which South ruffs. Declarer now leads the ♡ K. It does not help West to win and force again in diamonds. He must duck and South must switch at once to spades. Again West must hold up the Ace. When he wins the next spade the position is:

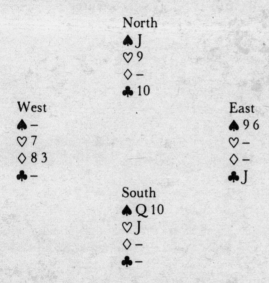

```
                    North
                    ♠ J
                    ♡ 9
                    ◊ -
                    ♣ 10

        West                        East
        ♠ -                         ♠ 9 6
        ♡ 7                         ♡ -
        ◊ 8 3                       ◊ -
        ♣ -                         ♣ J

                    South
                    ♠ Q 10
                    ♡ J
                    ◊ -
                    ♣ -
```

The next diamond sinks the ship: South cannot succeed whether he ruffs in dummy or in his own hand.

Conceding a ruff-and-discard

North
♠ 8 7 2
♡ K J
♣ A Q 6 4 2
♣ A 6 3

West
♠ 10 4
♡ A Q 9 4 3
◇ 8 3
♣ Q J 10 9

East
♠ 9 6 5
♡ 8 6 2
◇ K J 10 7
♣ 8 7 4

South
♠ A K Q J 3
♡ 10 7 5
◇ 9 5
♣ K 5 2

South	North
1 ♠	2 ◇
2 ♠	4 ♠

The ♣ J is led.

South takes the opening trick in his own hand with the King. If he leads a heart at once he can organise a heart ruff and make ten tricks. However, at the table South led a diamond to the Queen and King. The ♣ A was knocked out and after crossing to hand with a trump South led a heart. West won, cashed ♣ Q, and judged the position to be:

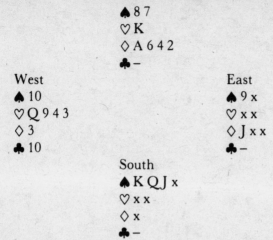

West knows that South is planning to ruff a low heart. So, why not let him ruff a club instead? If you examine the alternatives you will see that this is a winning defence. If dummy discards, East will throw a heart; if dummy ruffs, East will overruff and by the time South has overruffed and negotiated a ruff in hearts, West's ♠ 10 will be promoted.

DEFENCE AGAINST DECEPTIVE PLAY

Two examples follow where correct card-reading will nullify a clever trap set by the declarer.

Students of the game will recognise the point of the next deal:

North
♠ 6 4 3
♡ 7 5 2
♦ A Q 10 8 3
♣ Q 10

West
♠ K Q 10 9 2
♡ J 8
♦ 5 2
♣ J 9 6 2

East
♠ 7 5
♡ K Q 10 6 3
♦ K 7 6
♣ 5 4 3

South
♠ A J 8
♡ A 9 4
♦ J 9 4
♣ A K 8 7

South	North
1NT	2NT
3NT	

The ♠ K is led.

The normal play would be a low spade from South, heart switch, contract two down. But a clever South plays the ♠ J at trick one. Reading the declarer for A J alone, West eagerly leads a second spade. When he comes in with ♦ K, East has no spade to play.

We comment only that this defence, written up in so many magazine articles, would not succeed against a pair using the signal we have described. What is East doing with 8 7 5, West will ask himself. The 7 is an impossible card, so someone is lying and it can only be South.

Here, too, the declarer's deception is easily countered:

North
♠ A 10
♡ 10 9 7 6
◇ K J 10 5
♣ 10 8 6

West
♠ K 5 2
♡ J 5
◇ 9 8 6 3
♣ K Q J 2

East
♠ Q 9 7 6 4
♡ Q 4 2
◇ 7 4
♣ 7 5 4

South
♠ J 8 3
♡ A K 8 3
◇ A Q 2
♣ A 9 3

South	North
1NT	2♣
2♡	3♡
4♡	

West leads the ♣ K and wins the trick. He continues with the Queen, which South heads with the Ace. South draws two top trumps, then plays diamonds in the following manner: Ace, King, Jack from dummy. If East thinks that South began with ◇ A x and is about to take a ruffing finesse, he will discard rather than ruff with his winning trump. Then ◇ Q wins and declarer crosses to dummy for a discard on the fourth diamond. Of course, defenders who signal their distribution will not fall into this trap. East will know from the play of ♣ Q that his partner has four clubs, and from the high-low signal in diamonds that West has four diamonds.

PREPARING A DEFENCE AGAINST END-PLAY

Avoid the throw-in

Elimination and throw-in can be avoided in two ways: either by a defender refraining from winning a trick that would put him in the lead, or by unblocking a card that might result in a throw-in.

In the following example the moves to counter elimination and throw-in occur in the same suit.

                    North
                    ♠ Q 9 4 2
                    ♡ 10 8 6 3
                    ◊ Q
                    ♣ 7 5 4 2

West   East
♠ 7   ♠ 8 3
♡ K 9 7   ♡ Q 5 2
◊ J 10 9 8 4 2   ◊ A K 7 6 5
♣ K J 6   ♣ 10 9 3

                    South
                    ♠ A K J 10 6 5
                    ♡ A J 4
                    ◊ 3
                    ♣ A Q 8

        South   North
        2 ♠   2NT
        3 ♠   4 ♠

West leads the ◊ 10. East wins with the King and switches to ♣ 10. South goes up with the Ace and cashes the Ace and Queen of trumps, on which East plays the 8 followed by the 3. The ♡ 3 is led from dummy, East plays the 2, South the Jack and West ... well, what does West play?

It should be fairly plain to West that if he wins with the ♡ K he will have no good return. Partner's high – low in trumps indicates one even, three odd, and his lead of ♣ 10 means 10 9 x, not Q 10 9 (from which the 9 would be led). So West should be able to read the situation:

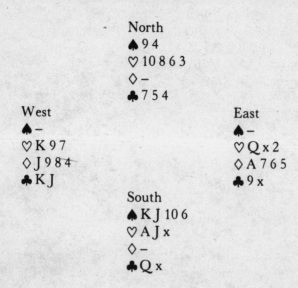

North
♠ 9 4
♡ 10 8 6 3
◇ –
♣ 7 5 4

West
♠ –
♡ K 9 7
◇ J 9 8 4
♣ K J

East
♠ –
♡ Q x 2
◇ A 7 6 5
♣ 9 x

South
♠ K J 10 6
♡ A J x
◇ –
♣ Q x

West defeats the contract by allowing ♡ J to hold and then unblocking the King if South continues with the Ace. Should South instead play clubs, West, winning the trick, switches to hearts.

The key to this sparkling defence lies in the information West has received on the pattern of the concealed hands, which excludes the possibility of South holding one of these hands:

(1)
♠ A K J 10 6 5
♡ A J
◇ x 3
♣ A Q x

(2)
♠ A K J 10 6 5
♡ A Q J
◇ 3
♣ A x x

It would be right in both cases for West to take the ♡ K and switch to diamonds in alternative (1) and clubs in alternative (2).

Mistaken policy by the defenders often assists the declarer to bring off an elimination end-play.

North
♠ 10 9 5
♡ K 5 4 2
◊ 10 3 2
♣ 7 6 5

West
♠ Q 7 3
♡ 3
◊ A K J 9 4
♣ K J 4 2

East
♠ J 8 6 2
♡ 9 8
◊ Q 8 7 5
♣ 9 8 3

South
♠ A K 4
♡ A Q J 10 7 6
◊ 6
♣ A Q 10

West	North	East	South
1 ◊	pass	pass	4 ♡

The ◊ K is led.

Seeing his partner's 8 at trick one, West tries a low diamond, hoping to put his partner in with the Queen. Declarer now has a simple line of play: he eliminates diamonds, plays Ace, King and another spade, and waits for a second trick in clubs.

Now let us see what happens if the defenders are using counting leads and trick-counting signals. West's lead of ◊ K signifies five diamonds, so East, knowing that only one trick is available in the suit, plays his lowest card, the 5. Realising that a diamond continuation will help declarer to eliminate the suit, West switches to a heart. West later unblocks in spades. When he wins his first trick in clubs he is able to exit safely in diamonds.

Averting a squeeze

To defend against an impending squeeze it is necessary to be familiar with the mechanics of squeeze play, a subject outside the scope of this book. It is also necessary to exchange information about the lie of the cards. In this example East has a chance to destroy communications.

North
♠ A 7 3
♡ 10 3
◇ K J 7 4
♣ 6 5 4 2

West
♠ 6 4 2
♡ K Q J 9
◇ Q 6 5 3
♣ J 3

East
♠ K J 5
♡ 7 4 2
◇ 10 9 2
♣ Q 9 8 7

South
♠ Q 10 9 8
♡ A 8 6 5
◇ A 8
♣ A K 10

South	North
1NT	2NT
3NT	

The ♡ J is led.

South holds up the Ace. West continues with the Queen, showing an even number, and South wins the third round. A finesse of ♠ 10 loses to the Jack. Remembering that South has opened a strong no-trump, East can read the position exactly:

North
♠ A 7
♡ —
◇ K J 7 4
♣ 6 5 4

West
♠ x x
♡ K
◇ Q x x x
♣ J x

East
♠ K 5
♡ —
◇ 10 9 2
♣ Q 9 8 7

South
♠ Q 9 x
♡ 8
◇ A x
♣ A K x

The 'obvious' switch to a club enables South to squeeze West in the red suits. (The play goes: ♣ A, spade to King, ♣ K, spade to Ace, diamond to Ace, spade winner.) Instead, East must attack communications by leading ◇ 10 in the diagram position, and another diamond when he comes in with ♠ K.

A second line of defence is to prevent the declarer from establishing necessary menace cards.

North
♠ J 9 7 2
♡ 9 5 3
◇ A K 2
♣ K Q 9

West
♠ 5
♡ Q J 10 8 6 2
◇ 8 7 6 4
♣ 6 2

East
♠ 6 3
♡ 7 4
◇ Q 9 5 3
♣ A J 10 7 3

South
♠ A K Q 10 8 4
♡ A K
◇ J 10
♣ 8 5 4

South	North
2 ♠	3 ♠
4 ♠	5 ◇
5 ♡	6 ♠

The ♡ J is led.

South wins and draws trumps, West discarding ♡ 2, which shows that he now has an odd number. Declarer leads a club to the King, West playing the 6. If East wins South has all the conditions for a classic double squeeze. After dummy's top club has been played off, ♡ 9 will be a menace against West, ♣ 8 menace against East, with diamonds as the pivotal suit which neither defender can guard.

As the cards lie, East can defeat the squeeze by holding up ♣ A. It would be wrong to suppose, however, that this hold-up would always be correct. Suppose West had played ♣ 2 on the first round of clubs, indicating an odd number: then it would be necessary to win and return a club to prevent a throw-in. As so often, careful use of signals is the key to accurate defence.

Sometimes it is wrong to lead an apparently safe card because you may need this card later on.

```
                        North
                        ♠ 10 8 4 2
                        ♡ J 6
                        ◇ K 8 5
                        ♣ A 7 6 3
      West                                East
      ♠ 6 5 3                             ♠ A K Q J
      ♡ 7 4                               ♡ 8 5 3
      ◇ Q 10 6 4                          ◇ A 9 7 2
      ♣ 10 9 5 4                          ♣ 8 2
                        South
                        ♠ 9 7
                        ♡ A K Q 10 9 2
                        ◇ J 3
                        ♣ K Q J
```

East	South	West	North
1 ♠	3 ♡	pass	4 ♡

The ♠ 3 is led.

East wins the first two tricks in spades, discovering that West holds three. A third spade may seem completely safe, but in fact it would be a mistake. The ending is difficult to foresee, even for a player with a good understanding of squeeze play, but the spade continuation can achieve nothing and in fact allows South to play a fourth spade when in dummy with ♡ J. The result is seen when this ending arises:

North
♠ –
♡ –
◊ K 8
♣ A 7 6 3

West
♠ –
♡ –
◊ Q 10
♣ 10 9 5 4

East
♠ –
♡ –
◊ A 9 7 2
♣ 8 2

South
♠ –
♡ 10
◊ J 3
♣ K Q J

Now the ♡ 10 forces West to discard a diamond.* This would not matter if East, when he won with ◊ A, still held a master spade.

As all squeeze practitioners know, a squeeze is usually effective when declarer can win 'all the remaining tricks but one'. There is an art in not allowing this situation to arise.

* This is described as a 'Vice' squeeze in Terence Reese's book, *The Expert Game*

North
♠ 10 9 4
♡ A K 7 3
◇ A Q 5
♣ A Q 8

West   East
♠ K Q J 7   ♠ A 6 2
♡ Q 9 8 5 2   ♡ 10 6
◇ 8 2   ◇ J 10 9 3
♣ 6 2   ♣ J 10 7 4

South
♠ 8 5 3
♡ J 4
◇ K 7 6 4
♣ K 9 5 3

North	South
1 ♡	1NT
3NT	

The ♠ J is led.

West holds the first trick and continues with the Queen, indicating an even number. As he guards both minors, East can see that a discard on the fourth round of spades will be embarrassing. He can let go a heart, perhaps, but then two top hearts will compel him to discard again. To prevent this situation from arising East allows ♠ Q to hold, blocking the suit. When in on the third round East switches to the ◇ J. The declarer may now try four rounds of diamonds, but East can escape by exiting with a *low* club.

PART FOUR

The Last Ditch

We have studied middle-game positions where an end-play can be averted, and now we consider possible defensive manoeuvres when the end-play is imminent.

ELIMINATION AND THROW-IN

The commonest form of end-play is a throw-in that compels a defender to lead into a tenace or concede a ruff-and-discard. Sometimes the lead into a tenace does not cost.

```
                    North
                    ♠ 9 8 7 5
                    ♡ 9 8 5
                    ◇ A J 10 4
                    ♣ 7 3

    West                            East
    ♠ 4                             ♠ 10 6 3
    ♡ Q 10 7 6 4                    ♡ 2
    ◇ 9 8 6 3                       ◇ K Q 7
    ♣ 9 5 4                         ♣ A K Q 8 6 2

                    South
                    ♠ A K Q J 2
                    ♡ A K J 3
                    ◇ 5 2
                    ♣ J 10
```

South	West	North	East
1 ♠	pass	2 ♠	3 ♣
4 ♠			

The ♣ 4 is led.

East takes two club tricks and switches to the ♡ 2. South takes the Ace and West plays the 4. South continues with ♠ A K Q, West discarding the ♡ 6 and the ♣ 9. South then leads a diamond to the 10 and King. East has the count and should see that a return of ◊ Q will give declarer an immediate trick, but not a vital one, as partner will still make the ♡ Q.

What happens if East instead returns a club, conceding a ruff-and-discard in this position?

North
♠ 9
♡ 9 8
◊ A J 4
♣ –

West
♠ –
♡ Q 10 7
◊ 9 8 3
♣ –

East
♠ –
♡ –
◊ Q 7
♣ K 8 6 2

South
♠ J 2
♡ K J 3
◊ 2
♣ –

Obviously the declarer can succeed if he ruffs out the ◊ Q, but in practice he does not even need to guess. He ruffs the club in his own hand, discarding a heart from dummy. And West? He is caught in a ruffing squeeze on this trick, forced to make a fatal discard either in hearts or diamonds.

Now make a slight change in the West and East hands, giving South a diamond more and a heart less:

North
♠ 9 8 7 5
♡ 9 8 5
◇ A J 10 4
♣ 7 3

West
♠ 4
♡ Q 10 7 6 4 3
◇ 9 8 6
♣ 9 5 4

East
♠ 10 6 3
♡ 2
◇ K Q 7
♣ A K Q 8 6 2

South
♠ A K Q J 2
♡ A K J
◇ 5 3 2
♣ J 10

After the same early play in Four Spades, East is on lead in this position:

North
♠ 9
♡ 9 8
◇ A J 4
♣ –

West
♠ –
♡ Q 10 7
◇ 9 8
♣ 9

East
♠ –
♡ –
◇ Q 7
♣ K 8 6 2

South
♠ J 2
♡ K J
◇ 3 2
♣ –

East sees the same cards as before, but the play this time has marked West with six hearts and three diamonds, not five hearts and four diamonds. Now the winning return is a club, conceding a ruff-and-discard. South has entry troubles and cannot take full advantage.

When a defender has to lead into a tenace in one suit or another, an accurate count may tell him which suit to choose.

North
♠ A 10 9 4 3
♡ A 10 9 6
◇ J 5
♣ J 4

West
♠ 6
♡ Q J 2
◇ K 9 6 2
♣ K 9 7 6 3

East
♠ 5 2
♡ 7 5 4
◇ 10 8 4 3
♣ 10 8 5 2

South
♠ K Q J 8 7
♡ K 8 3
◇ A Q 7
♣ A Q

South	North
2NT	3♣
3♠	4NT
5♡	6♠

West leads the ♠ 6.

South draws trumps and plays three rounds of hearts, producing this position, with West in the lead:

```
                    North
                    ♠ A 10 9
                    ♡ 10
                    ◇ J 5
                    ♣ J 4
West                                    East
♠ –                                     ♠ –
♡ –                                     ♡ –
◇ K 9 6 2                               ◇ x x x x
♣ K 9 7 6                               ♣ x x x x
                    South
                    ♠ J 8 7
                    ♡ –
                    ◇ A Q x
                    ♣ A Q
```

Which suit should West lead, and is there anything to guide him? Unfortunately East has been unable to signal his length in either diamonds or clubs. But East *has* been able to use the new trump signal. He has played 2 and 5 in trumps, indicating a hand with three even suits, one odd. West knows that East has three hearts, so he must be 4-4 in the minors. This solves West's problem, telling him to lead a club and wait for his diamond trick.

At no-trumps, also, a defender may have to choose whether to give up a trick by leading into one tenace or another.

North
♠ K 10
♡ 8 7 5
♢ A 10 9 7
♣ J 9 8 6

West
♠ Q J 9
♡ K Q 9
♢ J 6 5 3
♣ A Q 2

East
♠ 7 6 5 4 2
♡ 6 4 3 2
♢ Q 2
♣ 5 3

South
♠ A 8 3
♡ A J 10
♢ K 8 4
♣ K 10 7 4

South plays in 3NT after West has opened One Club.

West leads the ♠ Q. Dummy wins with the King, and the ♣ 9 goes to West's Queen. West continues with the ♠ J, which is allowed to hold the trick, and a third spade to the Ace. When South leads another club West goes up with the Ace and exits with a club. After a club to dummy and a heart to the 10 and Queen, the position is:

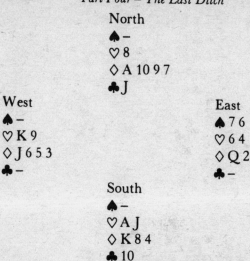

North
♠ –
♡ 8
◇ A 10 9 7
♣ J

West
♠ –
♡ K 9
◇ J 6 5 3
♣ –

East
♠ 7 6
♡ 6 4
◇ Q 2
♣ –

South
♠ –
♡ A J
◇ K 8 4
♣ 10

What should West lead now? A heart or a diamond? He will not know the answer unless East has given him a clue to the distribution. By playing high-low in hearts East shows an even number. This tells West that a heart return is relatively safe, because it will give up only one trick, whereas a diamond may surrender two tricks.

South, on the bidding, might have held instead:

♠ A 8 3
♡ A J 10 6
◇ K 8
♣ K 10 7 4

Now a heart return would give away two tricks, but a diamond gives up only one trick in this situation:

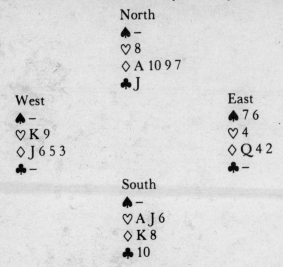

North
♠ –
♡ 8
◇ A 10 9 7
♣ J

West
♠ –
♡ K 9
◇ J 6 5 3
♣ –

East
♠ 7 6
♡ 4
◇ Q 4 2
♣ –

South
♠ –
♡ A J 6
◇ K 8
♣ 10

West has just won with the ♡ Q. Should he now return a
heart, South will win the contract. The correct card is the *Jack*
of diamonds. A low diamond, whether or not East contributes
the Queen, exposes West to a squeeze in diamonds and hearts
(e.g. ◇ 10 holds, diamond to King, club to Jack).

SQUEEZE AND PSEUDO-SQUEEZE

On many deals the declarer will have a choice between a
squeeze and a finesse. Good discarding at an early stage may
cause him to take the wrong decision. The secret is to unguard
honours *before* this is necessary.

North
♠ A Q 10 8
♡ A 8 4
◇ 4 2
♣ K J 10 4

West
♠ 9 5 3 2
♡ J 10 9 7 5
◇ A 10
♣ 5 3

East
♠ K J 6
♡ Q 3
◇ J 9 8 7 6
♣ 8 6 2

South
♠ 7 4
♡ K 6 2
◇ K Q 5 3
♣ A Q 9 7

South	North
1 ◇	1 ♠
1NT	3NT

The ♡ J is led.

East covers with the Queen, holding the trick, and returns the suit. There is something to be said for winning in dummy and leading a diamond (attacking the entries of the danger hand), but needing to develop just one extra trick South may win the second heart with the King and finesse ♠ 10. East switches to diamonds and a few tricks later the following situation is reached, with the lead in dummy:

North
♠ A Q
♡ A
◇ –
♣ 10

West
♠ 9 5
♡ 10 9
◇ –
♣ –

East
♠ K 6
♡ –
◇ 8 7
♣ –

South
♠ 7
♡ 6
◇ 5
♣ A

It is natural for East to discard a diamond on ♡ A, but East can see he is going to be squeezed on the next lead and psychologically it is better to bare ♠ K on the present trick. Good players, looking ahead, often unguard Kings and Queens several tricks before the ultimate pressure is applied.

Innumerable contracts are made because defenders unguard the wrong suits when no genuine squeeze exists. It is easy to see what might happen on the following deal:

North
♠ A 8 5
♡ 10 4
◇ A K 10 9 7
♣ K 6 4

West
♠ Q 10 3
♡ K Q J
◇ 8 6 5 2
♣ 5 3 2

East
♠ J 7 2
♡ 8 7 5 3 2
◇ 4
♣ J 10 9 7

South
♠ K 9 6 4
♡ A 9 6
◇ Q J 3
♣ A Q 8

South is playing 6NT, after a standard opening 1NT. West leads the ♡ J, which is allowed to hold, and follows with the King (odd number in the suit). After four rounds of diamonds the position is:

North
♠ A 8 5
♡ –
◇ A
♣ K 6 4

West
♠ Q 10 3
♡ Q
◇ –
♣ 5 3 2

East
♠ J 7 2
♡ –
◇ –
♣ J 10 9 7

South
♠ K 9 6
♡ 9
◇ –
♣ A Q 8

East has to discard on ◇ A. If he lacked information about the heart division East might let go a spade (which would be right if West had led from four hearts and South had none left). Thanks to the counting signal, East knows that South holds a menace card in hearts, the 9. If South holds ♣ A Q x x the contract cannot be defended, because any discard by East will be fatal. East must assume that South has only three clubs and must discard a club on ◇ A. To throw a spade would expose West to an eventual squeeze in spades and hearts.

PART FIVE

Examples of Combined Defence

We conclude with some examples of combined defence made possible only by the use of signals and fine deduction.

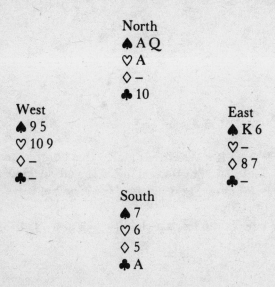

```
                    North
                    ♠ A Q
                    ♡ A
                    ◇ –
                    ♣ 10

West                                    East
♠ 9 5                                   ♠ K 6
♡ 10 9                                  ♡ –
◇ –                                     ◇ 8 7
♣ –                                     ♣ –

                    South
                    ♠ 7
                    ♡ 6
                    ◇ 5
                    ♣ A
```

It is natural for East to discard a diamond on ♡ A, but East can see he is going to be squeezed on the next lead and psychologically it is better to bare ♠ K on the present trick. Good players, looking ahead, often unguard Kings and Queens several tricks before the ultimate pressure is applied.

Innumerable contracts are made because defenders unguard the wrong suits when no genuine squeeze exists. It is easy to see what might happen on the following deal:

North
♠ –
♡ 9 8
◊ K
♣ K 7 3 2

West   East
♠ –   ♠ J 7
♡ A J 6 5   ♡ 3
◊ 10   ◊ –
♣ Q 10   ♣ J 9 6 4

South
♠ 10 9
♡ K 4
◊ –
♣ A 8 5

When South leads ♣ 5 West must realise that South is going to attempt to end-play him by cashing ◊ K and ducking the next round of clubs (or finessing the Jack if he holds it). So West plays ♣ Q on this trick.

Two tricks later South leads a club from dummy. Now it is East's turn to shine:

North
♠ –
♡ 9 8
◊ –
♣ 7 3 2

West   East
♠ –   ♠ J
♡ A J 6 5   ♡ 3
◊ –   ◊ –
♣ 10   ♣ J 9 6

South
♠ 10
♡ K 4
◊ –
♣ A 8

To thwart the declarer's intention to duck and end-play West, East completes a brilliant defence by playing the ♣ J.*

North
♠ Q 7 6 5 4
♡ J 9 7 6
◇ 5
♣ K 5 3

West
♠ K 3 2
♡ 8 3
◇ K J 6 3
♣ Q J 8 7

East
♠ J
♡ A Q 10 4
◇ 10 9 8 4 2
♣ 6 4 2

South
♠ A 10 9 8
♡ K 5 2
◇ A Q 7
♣ A 10 9

South	North
1NT	2 ♣
2 ♠	3 ♠
4 ♠	

The ♡ 8 is led.

Dummy plays the 9 and East the 10, since the lead marks South with K x x, not K x alone. South plays ♠ A and ♠ 10 and West is on lead in this position:

---

* Called the 'crocodile coup' because East must open his jaws like a crocodile to swallow his partner's 10.   T.R.

North
♠ Q 7 6
♡ J 7 6
◇ 5
♣ K 5 3

West
♠ 3
♡ 3
◇ K J 6 3
♣ Q J 8 7

East
♠ –
♡ A Q 4
◇ 9 8 4 2
♣ 6 4 2

South
♠ 9 8
♡ 5 2
◇ A Q 7
♣ A 10 9

If South held ♡ A and East ♣ A 10 x a switch to ♣ Q would be best, but East has assisted his partner to the right decision by throwing ◇ 10 on the second round of trumps. This can only be a suit preference signal, so West leads a second heart. East cashes Ace and Queen and leads a fourth round to kill the discard. South ruffs and after a spade to the Queen these cards are left:

North
♠ 7 6
♡ –
◇ 5
♣ K 5 3

West
♠ –
♡ –
◇ K J 3
♣ Q J 7

East
♠ –
♡ –
◇ 9 8 2
♣ 6 4 2

South
♠ –
♡ –
◇ A Q 7
♣ A 10 9

The defenders are not out of the wood by any means. On the next spade East, realising that his partner is going to come under pressure in the minor suits, must discard a diamond: his ♣ 6, which beats dummy's 5, is a highly valuable card. South throws a club and West, who knows the count from his partner's play in diamonds (the second and third cards were high-low) must trust his partner to hold a guard in clubs. After this careful play by the defence South must lose another trick.

In this final example an unusual communication play is made possible by the exchange of signals:

```
                    North
                    ♠ A J 5 2
                    ♡ A 10 8
                    ◊ K Q 8
                    ♣ K 7 3
West                                    East
♠ K 9 3                                 ♠ Q 10 7 6
♡ 7 2                                   ♡ 6 5 3
◊ A 9 5 3                               ◊ J 2
♣ J 9 6 5                               ♣ A 8 4 2
                    South
                    ♠ 8 4
                    ♡ K Q J 9 4
                    ◊ 10 7 6 4
                    ♣ Q 10
```

North	South
1NT	2♣
2♠	3♡
4♡	

West leads the ♡ 2.

South wins the first trick and plays a diamond to the Queen. East is not sure that he can spare the Jack so he plays the 2. Two more trumps follow and West has to find a discard.

East's play in trumps has indicated one odd suit, three even. His trumps are the odd suit and there are clues to his exact distribution. He must hold four spades (since South did not raise spades) and his play of ◊ 2, denoting an even number, must signify two diamonds, not four. Already the entire hand pattern is clear. West at this point can afford either a spade or a club. He throws a spade on the third round of hearts and a club when declarer plays a fourth round. East also throws a club on this trick. After a diamond to the King the position is:

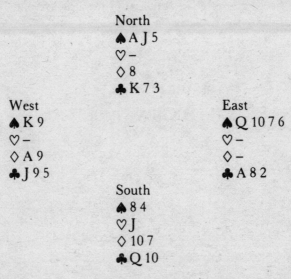

North
♠ A J 5
♡ –
◊ 8
♣ K 7 3

West
♠ K 9
♡ –
◊ A 9
♣ J 9 5

East
♠ Q 10 7 6
♡ –
◊ –
♣ A 8 2

South
♠ 8 4
♡ J
◊ 10 7
♣ Q 10

Declarer leads a low club from dummy. If the ♣ Q wins this trick South will play his last trump and no defence will succeed against best play. However, East also has a complete picture of the distribution. His partner's play in the trump suit has shown three even suits, one odd suit, and the discard of ♠ 3 means that the odd suit is spades. East must obviously place his partner with the ♠ K, and on this assumption the ♣ A, followed by a low spade to the King and Ace, is a promising and, as it turns out, a winning defence.

INDEX

ABOUT THE AUTHOR

In 1959 the publication of *The Distribution Signal*, by Helge Vinje, aroused considerable attention. This book, in fact, introduced an entirely new approach to defensive play, based on the exchange of information by signalling. The new theories had been developed by the author and other members of the Academic Bridge Club at the University of Oslo.

This brief survey of past events had a two-fold purpose; first to identify Vinje's theories on signalling, based on the two-card difference principle, and further developed in his new book; secondly, to show that these ideas have already proved sufficiently attractive and advanced to be adopted on a worldwide scale.

However, whereas Vinje's first book dealt primarily with distribution signals, his theories have now been enlarged to encompass the entire area of signalling technique. This new book will be welcomed on all sides as a landmark in the development of defensive play.

ABOUT THE EDITOR

Terence Reese was born at Epsom England, in 1913 and learned to play bridge at the age of seven. He was top scholar of Bradfield College and top classical scholar of New College, Oxford. After working at Harrods for a year he made bridge his career. As a player he has won every honour in the game, including the world championship. He has been bridge correspondent of the *Observer*, the *Evening News*, and the *Lady* for thirty years and is the author of fifty books on bridge, poker, canasta, backgammon, and casino gambling, including the autobiographical *Bridge at the Top*. Mr. Reese is married and lives in Mayfair.